# Bring It On...
## We're in Our 70's

If you can remember psychedelic art
from the sixties but you can't remember
where you put your keys, you might be
between the ages of 70-80

*Best Wishes !*

# Dedication

I dedicate this book to my late husband Steve and my kid brother Dan. Steve died at the age of 76 from Alzheimer's disease and complications from a stroke. Dan died at the age of 69. He never became a Septuagenarian.

# TABLE OF CONTENTS

# Preface

My dad died at the age of 35 and my mother died approximately 20 years later. I never thought I would live to be a Septuagenarian.  On my 70th birthday I realized not only did I live to be 70 years old, I hoped to live long enough to enjoy this decade to the fullest.

It was at that point I attempted to put my thoughts into writing about these years.  I started taking copious notes about the ideas and thoughts and shenanigans of my peers during my early seventies, however, this book took shape over a long period of time because at that time my full-time job was being a caregiver for my husband.

Steve was diagnosed with Alzheimer's disease shortly after my 70th birthday and along the way he had suffered three minor strokes. After he passed I started to organize all the notes about myself and my friends who were in their seventies. It was then that I began the process of writing this book.

One chapter led to another and not necessarily in any order were they written. There is much to be gained by reading about seventy-year olds and you do not have to be 70 to enjoy the characters.

I found that seventy-year olds and technology don't always mix, as you will discover when reading the chapter titled: "Catching Up With Technology – Whatever That Means".  I began to realize that parenting while in your 70s is not an easy task. And, I learned that most people in their seventies begin to formulate an "exit strategy".

When you read Bring It On…You're In Your 70's you will get a glimpse about how a lot of 70-year olds deal with their fears and their spiritual lives. You begin to realize they date and very often they re-invigorate their sexy self.

I tried to inject humor when the occasion would arise during my interviews and I have highlighted the start of each chapter with a joke.

If you find things in the book to be irrelevant then I probably haven't presented it well enough. I can say with honesty that I could go on and on and write more and more about the lucky ones who are living as Septuagenarians, but I decided to finish the book with the chapter about widowhood and leave the rest of the writing to the imagination and the recollection of my readers.

I am sure each and every one of you could add a paragraph or two while immersing yourself in this book. In fact, you might want to write your own anecdotes in the margins.

It's been an adventure that I am glad to have had the opportunity to share with you. I think you will enjoy reading "Bring It On…We're In Our 70's as much as I did writing about these 70-year olds.

# Chapter 1

# Getting Old is a One-Time Experience

When you're 70 years old, you become more thankful for "the big things in life." For example, large print crossword puzzles.

**D**id you know that growing old is a one-time experience? And, you do realize there is only one choice to NOT growing old? What defines getting old? Is it the span of time you have lived or, is it how your body looks and functions or is it the way you feel?

If you are not yet a Septuagenarian, you probably know people who are. Perhaps your parents or grandparents are in their seventies and you are reading this book to better understand where they are coming from. Maybe you are fast approaching this age group and want to sneak a peek at what the book says. Or, hopefully you are between the ages to 70-80 and are reading this book for the sake of finding out that you have a lot in common with others in your age group.

The "all knowing" Wikipedia search describes a 70-year-old as a Sep-tu-a-ge-nar-i-an.... A Septuagenarian is a person who is 70 years old or.... between the ages of 70 and 80. Yes, it did hit me that I am getting old. After all, if Wikipedia says it is so, then it is so. Right?

I have interviewed many 70-80-year-old men and women – technically known as Septuagenarians. A lot of the women see the wrinkles, gray hair, sagging skin, loss of muscle tone, and a few extra pounds that were not there when they were 25. Most of them were at a loss as to when all these changes took place. Menopause has come and gone and with it our young, strong, and flexible bodies.  I observed a lot of the men who experienced physical changes as well. They are sporting big guts and bald heads. Now we understand why there are "cougars".

When I was in my early 70s I thought "Oh my God, I'm really old but I don't feel old". I recall not feeling much older than when I was 50. Maybe that is why they are saying the seventies are like the new fifties.

When I was celebrating my 70th birthday I remember saying, bring it on-I'm in my 70s. I guess that was when I began formulating this book.

I found a quote on Facebook from a friend who had just turned 70 that was worth repeating. Since I copied this from Facebook, I will put it in italics:

*"What they bring to the table with their youth and zest for life, we bring with our wisdom, experience, and good hearts. For all we've been through earning each gray hair ... raising kids, bills and illnesses, and whatever else life brought you/us over the 30's, 40's, 50's, & 60's, we are survivors ... we are warriors ... we are women. Like a classic car or fine wine. While our exterior may not be what it once was, it is traded for our spirit, our courage, and our strength to enter this chapter of our lives with grace and pride for all we've been*

*through and accomplished. Never feel bad about aging. It is a privilege denied to many."*

*Ladies, I challenge you to repost with your picture and age.*

I loved that post from Facebook and it certainly rings true for a lot of women and men too who have celebrated their 70th birthdays.

Here's what they tag on next to the word Septuagenarian: golden ager, old person, oldster, senior citizen. Aw, come on Wikipedia, do I really have to be called these names any longer? Some people that I talked to said they preferred being called "a classic". Wait a minute, even that sounds old to me.

Now that I have an official description, I think I will just refer to all of us as Septuagenarians. In that manner, I will not have to focus on each year per se. From now on I will just say my age is between 70 and 80. Yes, that ought to do it. Done. Now I feel better.

However, people probably won't call me a Septuagenarian. What do I want to be called is the question? I guess I still want to be called by my name which is exactly what people have been calling me all my life. Yep, that's what I want to be called – just plain Bea. Most people said they prefer to be called by their given names. When people say, "hey Bea", I will turn around and smile, but if they insist on referring to me as "ma'am" perhaps I will simply ignore them. Why do I find being called "ma'am" so offensive? Hmmm.

Since most people will not call me a Septuagenarian, I wonder what they will call me. I suppose I am being called all the things that I never wanted to hear myself being called like senior citizen, or an older person, or ma'am.

I don't know why we are so concerned about what we want to be called at this age, but it has become an obsession with a lot of those that I interviewed. When some inquisitive person asks my age, I will answer them with a smile and say, "I am Bea, a Septuagenarian". Wow, I'm glad we got that straightened out!

I heard it said that the seventies are the new fifties. But, let's face it. 70 still reeks of old age, and that seems to be what most people I interviewed for this book are dealing with. On the other hand, a lot of Septuagenarians that I interviewed said they thought of the 80s and 90s as old age because they were still feeling young. Obviously old age is relative.

One person I interviewed told me a story about when she realized she was getting old. She was in her 70s and was talking to her son shortly after his 50th birthday. He said, "Mom, I am really mad". When she asked why he replied, "I went to the movies yesterday and they asked me if I wanted the senior discount!" She said she laughed out loud and asked him, "How do you think that makes me feel?" Having a kid who is being asked if they want a senior discount at the movies will surely make you feel old. Oh, the life of the Septuagenarian.

Ann, another Septuagenarian, tells me her son makes her feel old in an unusual sort of way. She explains that every year when he calls to wish her a happy birthday he says, "Mom,

4

you are the oldest mom I have". She says he has been saying that same thing since she was in her 40s.

When I interviewed Margie, she said, the thing that makes her feel old is listening to music from the 50s and 60s. While remembering the words to all the hit songs from those years, she says she does not understand the words to anything she hears on the radio these days.

I heard a lot of complaints from 70-year olds about the things they no longer can do with ease. Things like climbing a ladder to change a light bulb in the ceiling, hanging a picture, moving furniture, trying to unscrew the lid on a jar, or opening some of the prepackaged foods. Some people said that they rely on their children or grandchildren to help. But if you live alone with no one you can call on for help you better have the name and number of a good handyman.

Even with the challenges most Septuagenarians face they still stay active in many ways. Pickleball is very popular among seniors as is golf, tennis, swimming and hiking. I also know Septuagenarians who are good Texas hold'em players and all the other crazy games of Poker they seem to enjoy.

Most people interviewed while writing this book have been very sure of one thing. They are trying to be self-sufficient in most everything they do and would like to think they will continue to be active and independent.

Several of the women I interviewed say getting dressed seems to take longer than what it used to. One gal told me she used to be able to hop in the shower and dress and be out of the house in about ½ hour and now she estimates at least one hour for this task. And, she says, "If I'm getting dressed for a special occasion and need to take more time on my makeup, I probably will need at least an hour and a half." I did not ask this question from any of the men I talked to.

Most everyone interviewed while writing this book have been very sure of one thing. They are happy to be independent in most everything they do and would like to think that they will continue to be independent.

Well, get ready for the ride. You just might look forward to traveling through these years after reading this book. Bring It On....We're in our 70's seems to be the prevailing attitude with the seventies crowd.

Chapter Two

# Are You "Silent" or "Booming"?

When Einstein was a young boy, he was a late talker and naturally his parents were worried. Finally, one day at supper, he broke into speech with the words "Die zuppe is tzu heiss." (The soup is too hot). His parents were greatly relieved but asked him why he hadn't spoken up to that time. The answer came back: "Bisher war alles in ordnung." (Until now everything was in order.)

$S$afe, silent and sometimes boring –that is one way to describe the Silent Generation while the Baby Boomers were known as the "me generation". Half of today's Septuagenarians are from the "silent generation" and the other half are "baby boomers" This makes for a very interesting mixture of 70-year olds.

If you were born in 1940 you are caught up in the tail end of the Silent Generation and the beginning of the Baby Boomers. The Silent Generation refers to people who were born between 1925 and 1945. The Baby Boomers followed the Silent Generation and typically their birth years begin from the early- to mid-1940s and ending anywhere from 1960 to 1964.

So, no matter which half you are in I'm sure you will remember "bee hive" hairdos and "leisure suits",

I am surprised to learn most 70-year olds did not end up cross eyed from watching that stupid Atari game called Pong. We sure did spend a lot of time watching the ping pong ball bounce back and forth on the early computers. I guess it didn't take much to entertain us back then. That was around 1975.

Forty some years later I am amazed to find that a lot of 70 year olds still do not know how to use a computer although, I must say, they are trying. You will read more about seniors and technology in a later chapter.

Most Septuagenarians feel they have lived in the very best of times – everything from watching Howdy Doody on a black and white 8" TV screen to watching Neil Armstrong land on the moon on their beautiful wooden TV cabinets with a 21" color screen. Today's 70 year olds watch TV on their 52" flat screens with more channels than they will ever have time to explore. Television first came on the market during the mid 40's spanning the silent generation and giving birth about the same time the Boomers were being born.

As these two overlapping generations think back to the invention of black and white television they are stunned to learn that doctors are now able to operate with a computer robot using a TV screen to see where they are inside the body.

When asked what kind of activities these 70-year olds experienced as a child I got nostalgic responses from almost everyone. They remembered playing hopscotch, jump rope, sand lot baseball and stickball. Most of the men recalled playing marbles, kick the can, mumbly peg and pitching pennies.

8

Riding their bikes all over town was the mode of transportation for most of them. They roller skated, ice skated, walked on stilts and hopped on their pogo sticks. They played hide and seek and tag and everyone remembered playing jacks and pick-up sticks. They had fond memories how they played outside with their neighborhood friends from dusk to dawn and only came home when it was nearing bath and bedtime. Some even recalled catching lightning bugs in their pajamas.

Most of them made comments regarding the young kids today who seem to have a constant head down gait.... meaning their heads are always looking at their cell phones even when they are walking. Seems as though their grandchildren's biggest activity is using their thumbs to text. Can you imagine how many of these kids will have arthritis in their thumbs when they become Septuagenarians?

When I asked what kind of media they enjoyed while growing up a few of them said they remembered that way back then the only media available was the radio and the Saturday afternoon news reel while at the movies. They remembered the family gathered around the radio and listened to their favorite radio shows together. Some radio shows that were remembered were The Fat Man, Fibber McGee & Molly, The Goldberg's, Amos and Andy, and Inner Sanctum. I'm sure if you are reading this and you are in your 70s or 80s you will recall a few more of your favorite radio shows.

One man, whom I interviewed, said his family got the first TV in the neighborhood he was only 8 years old. He remembered watching wrestling and Howdy Doody and Jack Benny and Ed Sullivan. He said that when there was nothing playing, he recalls watching the test tube pattern and snow. Another fellow I interviewed told me he used to climb up on the roof and turn the antenna when necessary.

I followed up with this question. What do you watch on your TV now? What did you consider to be your favorite series and what do you watch a lot of when you are watching television? Believe it or not, a lot of the women enjoyed the series called Sex and the City. They also enjoyed the cooking channel and House Hunters.

The men were very much in step with one another by watching sports, everything from football to golf and everything in between like basketball and even fishing. They even glued their eyes to WPT- World Poker Tour.

Both men and women admitted to watching too much of the 24-7 news channels and expressed their disgust with what they were getting from these sources. They reminisced what it was like before all the talking heads took over the news on cable TV. They liked it better when they were zoned into the 5:00 and the 11:00 news. They could watch one half hour and catch up with the local and national news, sports and weather and then get right back into their favorite sit-coms.

A big complaint among the 70-year olds that I talked to was the expense of keeping their cable service. Having a phone, an internet connection and cable TV was costing some Septuagenarians close to ¼ of what some were receiving from Social Security. Those that were struggling with this expense said they need this service so they can stay in touch with their grandchildren via Facebook, watch television and keep their phone service. At this early stage of streaming, most of the 70-year olds that I spoke with had never heard of Roku.

Nancy was not one of them. She was able to cut the cord with her cable television expense in a gradual manner. First, she had ROKU installed on her spare TV in her guest room. She told me it took her about two months before it got comfortable enough for her to realize she did not need cable to enjoy everything she was used to. At that point, she went out and bought the ROKU adaptor for her other two TV's. When Nancy told a few of her friends what she had done they told her she was a trendsetter and they wished they had to nerve to do this. Nancy told them when she converted to ROKU, she got the biggest pleasure out of cancelling with her cable company plus she could brag to her friends about all the money she was saving.

Another question asked during interviews was, what kind of games and activities do you participate in since you are no longer playing jump rope? Golf, Pickle ball, bowling, tennis and hiking were the most frequent answers when it came to physical activities. Cardio workouts and "senior splash" in the pool was another source of exercise. Of course, there was the usual card games…bridge, euchre, and poker. Mahjongg was taking hold to our seventy-year olds.

The children who grew up during this era worked very hard and kept quiet. It was commonly understood that children should be seen and not heard. I even read that is one of the reasons we are called the "silent generation".

There are several theories as to how the 'Silent Generation' originated. During this time, the House Committee on Un-

American Activities launched an assault on political freedom in America. This, in conjunction with Senator Joseph McCarthy's overzealous attempts to feed anti-communist sentiment in America, made it dangerous for people to speak freely about their opinions and beliefs. They became cautious about where they went and whom they were seen with. Therefore, the people were effectively 'silenced.'

In 1951, a *Time* magazine article was written in which the children of the generation were described as unimaginative, withdrawn, unadventurous, and cautious. *Time* magazine used the name 'Silent Generation' to refer to these individuals. The name has been there ever since.

When we were talking about this very thing, Dorothy told me she felt we were again being silenced by our government because you had to be careful what you said and make sure it was all very politically correct. Be PC or be quiet she said. So maybe this next generation will be called the PC or the quiet generation. Just saying.

Like the McCarthy era where it became dangerous to speak freely about opinions and beliefs makes it understandable to 70 somethings that being politically correct is the newest version of silencing. We are silent about admitting having ever used the N word, while blacks still call each other by the N word and that's ok. Let us remember, someone who had a profitable and popular cooking show on TV admitted to using the N word way back in her past and she was taken off the air and lost millions of dollars in income. So, it seems to me that those who were born in the silent generation are still being silenced with a world full of political correctness.

I read on the internet that there are approximately 49 million of us who are said to be members of the silent generation. I'm sure that number has diminished a bit since I wrote this. We did not have to struggle through the Depression, nor did we have to fight in World War II. I noticed the more I talked to late Septuagenarians, 75-80-year olds, clearly they wore the moniker of the "silent generation". They talked about their lives and seemed to enjoy doing so, both past and present.

Things were so peaceful during the silent generation when most Septuagenarians were growing up. And, most of today's "silent gens" wish they could still enjoy the same kind of peace of mind they felt while growing up. They did not have the 24-7 television news cycle agitating them day and night.

A lot of the Septuagenarians that I have interviewed feel that the world is upside down with unrest. Seems as though we have too much politically correctness and not enough honesty and forthrightness. We are clearly being indoctrinated to be PC even when it might not be expedient to be so.

We see this being done at every level of our lives. Obama felt that it is politically incorrect to use the word "terrorist" while his succeeding president Donald Trump tried to blame everything he could on the "terrorists". While Obama believed that if a bomb goes off under his butt by a radical Muslim, he probably still would not admit that it was a done by a radical Muslim terrorist while Trump is ready to blame everything on "illegal terrorists".

And, as if being silenced described the "silent generation", the booming voice of the other half of our described Septuagenarians, the "baby boomers" took center stage during and after Woodstock, the music and art festival in

1969. Boomers soon became known as the "counterculture" generation.

The "baby boomers", born between 1945 and 1964, still reminisce about Woodstock, and they have kept Birkenstock in business all these years. About 77 million Americans were born in this time period, making "boomers" significantly larger than the generations immediately before and after.

While interviewing some "boomers" it became apparent that change and conformance has not come easy for a lot of them. Mandy says she still is an active and vocal member of her political party and she went to the women's march in Washington DC. Barbara, who is an early Septuagenarian, spends a lot of time at political meetings and canvased door to door for Hillary in the 2016 election. Mandy and Barbara are just as fervent as 70-year olds as they were during the 1968 Chicago convention.

That convention gave us the Chicago eight consisting of protesters Abbie Hoffman, Tom Hayden, David Dellinger, Rennie Davis, John Froines, Jerry Rubin, Lee Weiner, and Bobby Seale. They were there to disrupt the convention with their demonstrations to end the war in Vietnam. I asked several women from the silent generation what they can remember about the 1968 Democratic convention and they said they can only remember changing diapers at that time in their life.

I was able to speak with a remnant from the "hippie" group of boomers. He still wears his long grey hair in a ponytail and is often seen wearing his Jerry Garcia tee shirt, or a tie dye shirt. When I interviewed him, I was surprised to hear that he is still very socially on the left but his basic voting philosophies are very much on the right.

I found that over and over again many "baby boomers" seemed to have shed their hippie label for a more conservative label. A good many of them have given up smoking hash and turned to cocktails instead. They gave up tie dye shirts for Brooks Brother's suits and the women started wearing bras.

Things were so peaceful during the silent generation when most Septuagenarians were growing up. And, most "silent gens" want to enjoy the same kind of peace of mind they felt while growing up. They did not have the 24-7 television news cycle agitating them day and night.

We Septuagenarians seem to have a much clearer understanding of religion, prejudice, racism and bigotry than many from the younger generations because we lived through it all.

Funny how, when Europeans immigrated, there were many roadblocks. A sponsor was needed, and you had to be medically fit in order to be accepted into this county.  And when you were accepted through the immigration process you were given a handshake and sent off to meet up with your sponsor. Nowadays, you can sneak into the country illegally, and instead of a handshake and a well wish, you get food stamps and free access to our schools and hospitals and jobs and a lot of other things – all at the expense of the American taxpayer. Some areas of the country even allow illegals to vote.

Whether you are a 'boomer' or a 'silent gen', most people I spoke with about immigration still hope and wish for immigrants to immerse themselves into the American culture however, they would like to see it done legally.

Are you a booming or are you a silent Septuagenarian? Are you boring beige or tie dye? Are you little black pumps or Birkenstocks? For those who have lived to become Septuagenarians they all agree… they are the luckiest generation to have experienced life no matter whether you are a "silent" or a "boomer".

Chapter 3

# Catching Up With Technology- Whatever That Means

Joe says that if he doesn't answer his phone when his Dad calls, Dad will leave a message that says: "Hello, it's Dad here, calling at 6:30pm on Monday, 15 March." I know Dad," Joe says to himself. My phone told me already.

That little joke recalls a lot of conversations I have had with 70 something's that speak volumes of them using their new-fangled cell phones. Or, at least their cell phone might be new to them. And, I might add, not only is a cell phone new to a lot of Septuagenarians, doing away with their land line phones and having to rely only on their cell phone is another story. In fact, I rue the day I got rid of my land line because now I am not able to call my cell phone in order to locate it when I forget where I have placed it. LOL

Annie's telephone tale is funny. She was so proud when she finally bought herself a brand new "smart" phone. She trotted off to the mall for her morning indoor walk with her new phone in hand. It rang. "OMG, what am I to do? Hello, hello, can you hear me" she said to the phone and it kept ringing. Push a button she thought, push a button. "Hello, hello" and then silence. The Smart Phone stopped ringing and in that very moment this Septuagenarian realized that the Smart

Phone made her feel not so smart. In fact, it made her feel stupid. She did not know how to answer her phone.

Annie was living in Florida, her family was up North, and she had no grandchildren close by, so what was she to do? Well, she looked up and right in front of her eyes was an AT&T store full of beautiful Smart phones and a very clean-cut young man alone in the store. It was still early, and the store had just opened so she walked in and looked him right in the eye and very boldly said, "I need to adopt a grandson, and I hope you will be him". She sheepishly told him, "I need to learn how to answer my new phone. Can you help me?" He smiled and said yes, he could help her. What is your phone number he asked? He called her right then and there and sure enough the phone rang, and he showed her how to swipe from left to right to answer. "Wow", she said, "why didn't I know that?"

Annie decided right then and there that she needed to adopt a grandchild and Tony, the 20 something salesman that helped her that day was going to be it. He took the time that morning to help her understand her new phone. Annie and Tony became friends and he opened the door for her to come in any time and he would help her learn how to navigate the functions of her new phone.

Annie's story had a happy ending. She was able to make a friend with a 20 something and get the help she needed.

Some of us were not so lucky to meet up with someone who could help us untangle technology and did not have a grandchild living close by.  Not only did we have the "newfangled" phones to deal, as we were needing help with our iPads, our tablets and our laptop computers.

I have talked to a lot of seventy-year olds about Smart phones and tried to figure out how much and how little they knew about this minicomputer. One Grandma I talked with had been using her cell phone for about three years and still did not know how to put someone on hold when another call was coming through. Don't laugh, this is more common than you might want to know.

I interviewed my friend Diane who did not have a computer, never used one and never wanted one but she seemed to be adept with her I Phone. She was very good with Facebook and instant messaging on her phone, so I asked her how she learned. You guessed it. She had her sixteen-year-old grandson for dinner once a week and over a period of time she learned to use some of the technology that was available to her on her phone like Facebook and messaging and dealing with her pictures. Her grandson set her up with an e-mail account however she says she has no use for that. The Facebook and the messaging and dealing with her pictures is the only "techy" stuff she wants to know.

Speaking about Cell phones, have you noticed that a lot of our grandchildren do not sit in front of the TV anymore? Most of the younger generations have their eyes glued to their phones and their thumbs are working a mile a minute while texting. Texting has become the new normal way of communicating and most Septuagenarians who have learned to text have found it difficult to grasp the acronyms such as LOL. LOL means laughing out loud. Then there is LMAO – laughing my ass off or ROTFL, rolling on the floor laughing. It goes on and on. In fact, these acronyms have almost become words in the new age of technology such as OMG for Oh my God. If someone asks you to meet them at 1:00 you should never say okay. Just type in the letter k. OMG, I'm LOL

Picture this when it comes to technology. An exasperated five-year-old talking to his Grandma. "No Grandma, listen. Double click the Internet Explorer Icon. Grandma listen…. the Icon is the picture of an e with a halo. Yes, Grandma, that's it."

Now, that just about explains computer technology for Septuagenarians. What is natural for a five year old when it comes to technology is a long way from being easy for a 70 year-old to understand, let alone learn. Words like icon, the cloud, double click, tweet, snap chat etc. are not everyday words in the language of most 70 year olds. Ask them to do a copy and paste and they might tell you they do not have a copier and what kind of glue should they buy.

You would be surprised how many seventy-year olds are still using the flip phone and I began to understand why. Yes, they are scared to death or just not able to understand the cell phones. It is hard for a lot of Septuagenarians to embrace any technology let alone stay abreast of the latest technologies. They don't understand what Wi-Fi is and what is does, and passwords become a real nightmare in the life of a Septuagenarian.

Most "Septy's" remember watching television when TV's first emerged in the late 40's. They watched Howdy Doody and wrestling and the Ed Sullivan show. When there was nothing to watch they recall sitting around the TV and watching the "snow" and the test tube pattern on their small black and white screens. My how things have changed.

If a family could afford to buy a television way back then, watching the channels were free. Now, we have cable television with hundreds of channels and the cost of watching is very often five times the cost that most 70-year olds pay for car insurance. A very big expense indeed for these folks who are on fixed incomes. And to make matters worse, the 70s crowd will be the last to give up their cable bill in lieu of Roku or Fire Stick, streaming and all the other new gadgets and methods that are out there so that they can eliminate the cost of cable. And, they are not ready to give up watching a movie on their TV screens in lieu of viewing a movie on their cell phones, computers or tablets. Doing away with cable seems like an unsurmountable task to go through. Just saying.

They tell me they have a comfort factor about watching TV that the younger generation does not have. The youngsters do not know nor need the comfort of a lounge chair for TV time as is the practice of Septuagenarians. Think about that, how many of these youngsters have seen their parents or grandparents fall asleep in front of the TV in their lounge chair. I don't think they want to be doing that while watching a show on their phone.

Another hard thing for a lot 70 somethings is how they do their banking in this age of electronics. Remember, a lot of them do not even own a computer let alone pay their bills on-line. If you can imagine this – they are still paying their bills with a check and licking a stamp and sending the check through the mails. I'll bet the banks are chomping at the bit for this generation of "tech-tards" to fade out so that ALL banking is done electronically.

One couple I spoke with told me they had a computer, did well keeping up with family by e-mails and Facebook but banking and writing bills scared them. They did not trust this method of paying bills. They finally concluded that it was something they needed to do. They went to the bank and said they wanted to learn how to pay their bills on line. The banker was very kind and considerate regarding their lack of confidence and showed them how to do it and how to set up an account, told them to pick a password and write it down so that they would remember it and off they went.

The banker helped them set up their account and helped them along for a few times and soon they were paying bills the same way their children and grandchildren were paying bills. They even learned how to transfer funds from savings to checking. Oh, how smug they were when they told me how adept they had become about bill paying. BTW, shortly before they began paying bills on-line, they bought a roll of stamps and at the rate they are paying on-line that roll of stamps will last them a lifetime.

Septuagenarians have chugged into the world of technology as late bloomers, but they are moving into the digital life and trying hard to catch up with their younger compatriots. The early 70-year olds (baby boomers) are more tuned into technology than the older Septuagenarians, (silent generation).

Martha told me the story about losing her job when the company she was with for the past 15 years went out of business. She tells me that she did not have a resume, did not know how to properly use e-mails to converse with hiring agents and she felt she was quietly being passed up by younger persons for the jobs that she was seeking. BTW, she was obligated to look for employment on a regular basis in order to collect her unemployment compensation. Martha went on to tell me that one hiring agent she talked to told her to e-mail her a short note about herself and attach her resume to the e-mail. She panicked. Martha confessed to me she did not know how to do an attachment on an e-mail and did not have a resume.

Can you imagine a 76-year-old looking for a job in this day and age? Yes, it certainly can be challenging for Septuagenarians to find a job but plenty of them do. Read my chapter on jobs for more information about this.

When visiting their doctors and the receptionist tells them they can get their results of testing by going to their portal – Wow, that's like the doctor's office telling them something in a foreign language. They do not know the meaning of a portal let alone try to read test results on line. They were much more used to hearing feedback from the doctor visit from their Doc. In my interviews with a lot of Septuagenarians I can say that this twenty-first century way of communicating with the medical profession is not going to be embraced by a lot of 70 somethings. Most of them say they still need the face to face encounters with their doctors. And, they went on to tell me this is not happening. A lot of doctor visits are being handled by the nurse practitioner and the doctor very often is incognito.

Of course, there is always the story of how some folks need to embrace technology as a means of survival in the business world.

When talking about technology I like to tell the story of my husband Steve. He was an architect and was a member of Mensa where he tested in the 99th percentile of the population. In other words, he was smart. He was an exception from someone born into the silent generation because he learned early on to embrace technology. He was self-taught in computers and learned to use the CAD (computer aided designs) programs. Because of that he was employable as an Architect when most in his age were not. I tell you Steve's story so that you will realize that had he not learned these computer skills while still in his fifties he would have been without a job long before retirement age.

A lot of the people I talked to tell me that they have forced themselves to learn and use the basic phone and computer skills for e-mails and Facebook and instant messaging in order to stay connected socially with their children and grandchildren. And, that seems to be the extent of their technology. They don't shop on line, or bank on line, and a lot of them do not have Wi-Fi in their homes. Seriously folks, that's just the way it is for a lot of Septuagenarians.

Most have skipped desk tops and laptops and went directly to cell phones and got a kindle to read on. That is the extent of their world when it comes to technology.

So, as most seventy-year olds feel the need to ask their children or grandchildren for help in understanding technology a lot of them expressed to me that it was embarrassing to admit they not only needed help, but they needed repetition in order to learn some of the technology that they were trying to catch on to.

My friend Joan told me that while asking for her son's expertise on a tech issue for the umpteenth time she noticed him rolling his eyes. I told him he needs "chill out" and understand my ignorance regarding this new technology and don't you dare roll your eyes every time I ask a question. Remember honey, I said, I was patient when I taught you how to do things like using a fork, getting dressed, combing your hair, tying your shoes and dealing with life's issues every day... and I did this with NO technology other than Dr. Seuss. When you realize how ignorant I am about technology today, you will see I'm getting old. I ask you to please be patient, but most of all, try to understand what I'm going through.

It is funny for us to watch our friends asking their phone questions and getting answers. They have embraced Google and Siri to the max.  For us, especially those of us from the silent generation, we still remember having to look things up in our Encyclopedia Britannica and today we simply ask Siri.

I am quite certain that is why, after 244 years of doing business, Encyclopedia Britannica has announced it is going out of print. And, that about sums up technology for a good many Septuagenarians.

Chapter 4

# The Donald and Hillary – 2016

Q:  If the Donald and Hillary are stranded on a boat in the middle of the ocean, who survives?

A:  AMERICA

I was seventy-six years old during the battle of the presidency between Donald Trump and Hillary Clinton – two very flawed candidates who left the country having to make a choice when voting for the President of the United States. One thing I can say for sure, no matter which of these two candidates win, the country will have a Septuagenarian serving as their president.

Our parents went through an election similar to the election of 2016 when the Chicago Tribune headline read: "Dewey Defeats Truman". It was an incorrect banner headline on the front page of the Chicago Daily Tribune on November 3, 1948, the day after incumbent United States President, Harry S. Truman, won an upset victory over Republican challenger and Governor of New York, Thomas E. Dewey, in the 1948 presidential election.  I was 8 years old at this time and I can still remember my parents' disappointment when they found out that Dewey did, in fact, lose that election.

The United States presidential election of 1948 is considered by most historians as the greatest election upset in American history. Virtually every prediction (with or without public opinion polls) indicated that incumbent President Harry S. Truman would be defeated by Republican Thomas E. Dewey. That is what was being said about the 1948 presidential election.

I wonder if the 2016 election might have surpassed the '48 election when it came to polling and predictions. Hillary Clinton was about to be named the first female president of the United States – all of the polling told us this and to the surprise of half of the country Donald Trump won. Trump got 304 Electoral votes to Clinton's 207. Donald Trump voters overwhelmingly took control of most of the country. But that is not the end of the story. The East and West coast voters came out in droves and Hillary Clinton came out ahead of Trump in the popular vote by nearly 3 million votes.

We already have learned that we Septuagenarians are divided by age groups making up the "silent generation" and the "baby boomers". And, after the election of 2016 we have come to realize we are divided by political party and ideology as evidenced by this election.

It seems as though half of the people I encountered while putting this book together were declared liberals and the other half claimed to be conservatives. Neither group of people liked each other, and they seemed to always be shouting at each other rather than talking.

When I was interviewing Maddie, I asked her why, at the age of 70, was she still showing her colors as a political activist. She told me she was out there knocking on doors trying to sell the voters on casting their vote for Hillary. She wanted to see a

woman in the White House. Maddie went on to tell me she
was always an activist. She marched in the 60's for segregation
and a million other causes. She told me she often took her
little children in their strollers on several marches.  Activism
was in her nature she said. I suggested to her that because of
the lack of enthusiasm on my part to vote for either one of
these flawed candidates I may not vote for the POTUS.
Maddie went on to say that women fought hard for the right
to vote and I should make a decision and cast my ballot for
one or the other. Hmmm.

I voted and Donald Trump won.

Barbara, a very classy and smart 74-year-old went to the
women's march in Washington, DC in 2017 with her grown
daughter as a protest against Donald Trump. The march was
held the day after his inauguration. I think that when I heard
this during one of my interviews, I realized the depth and the
dislike of the new president. His presidency divided the
parties and the liberals and the conservatives so deeply that
this divide may not be overcome in my lifetime. Just saying.

Anita, a diehard conservative, started out supporting Jeb in
the primary, and when he was knocked out of the running she
flipped her allegiance to Marco and soon that was no longer
an option. Finally, she settled on Ted Cruz and when he did
not win the primary she was devastated because she said she
would not vote for Hillary, but she had to hold her nose and
vote for the Donald.

Mary Beth thought it just might be refreshing to vote for
someone who says what's on his mind without worrying
about being politically correct about every last word that

comes out of his mouth or his tweets. Oh, how wrong she was. The established politicians, better known as the "Elite" were so upset about his winning that he could do nothing to satisfy any of them, both Democrats and Republicans.

Washington was going to be out to get Trump at all costs and Hillary was probably never going to be able to run for office again. The pundits on the talk shows were having a field day with their hatred for the newly elected President. And, Hillary was having a hard time getting over her loss.

Again, in my lifetime the only comparison to the 2016 POTUS election would have to be the Dewey-Truman election of 1948. The polls were wrong then and the polls were wrong regarding the Donald – Hillary election.

As a Septuagenarian, I can tell you that there probably wasn't a 70-year-old alive that did not have a strong opinion during this election. The most important thing that I learned was to try NOT to argue politics with any of my friends. And, when you read this chapter in the book you will probably have strong opinions about why I chose Trump over Clinton, but I was ready for a non-politician businessman to take the helm. Maybe I was right and maybe I was wrong but one thing I am sure of-The United States of America will survive.

# Chapter 5

# Crazy Career Changes and Challenges

I tried working in a muffler factory, but that was exhausting.

Then I tried to be a chef.  Figured it would add a little spice to my life, but I just didn't have the thyme.

Jack had a close friend who owned the busiest pawn shop in town and when he was in his seventies he was hired to be a greeter. What a hoot that was for Jack, being the gregarious guy that he was. As he told me in our interview, it sure beats being a greeter at Walmart.

When you look around many Walmart stores you might notice plenty of apparent Septuagenarians working as greeters.  Some of them are probably working because they need the money and some because they got just plain bored filling their days with TV and Golf.

After interviewing other Septuagenarians who are still working, I began to realize that there are a lot more 70 somethings who are working than what you might think. The fast food industry is being flooded with working seniors. Let's face it – who would you rather hire, a 70-year-old who has a decent, clean appearance who probably would be dependable, or, a youngster who has a face full of piercings and tattoos all over their bodies? The sad part of this is there are far too many Septuagenarians who need the added income to keep the roof over their heads or so they can afford their meds.

Denise, a very spunky widow, had the right idea. She got herself a part-time job selling men's clothing. She did this to meet men she told me. I think selling men's clothing might be more fun than selling furniture for that very reason.

I remember the day I was walking thru a high-end furniture store and saying to the salesman, "I don't suppose they would consider hiring a 76-year-old woman who has had a lot of experience in design and sales. Much to my surprise, he took my number and told the manager about me. I was blown away when I received a call from her the next day to come in – she wanted to talk to me. When I got the call, I almost forgot that I had asked for a job in a roundabout way.

I met the manager of the store the following day and we talked for almost an hour and to my surprise she said she would love to have me be part of the team. I told her I would only consider part time, three days a week, two eight-hour days and one 12-hour day and she agreed. I was excited to be getting back to the business that I knew and loved. Or, so I thought at the time. After reading the company manual and setting up my training days I was told that I had to work 4 days a week. It was then that I got hold of my ego about being hired at my age and started to realize I was not willing to put that much time and effort for a second chance at my career so I backed out of the offer. Oh well, I tried.

I talked to Maddie, a widow of two years, about her job. She was a former nurse and is now working part time in the wedding department at a large department store chain. Sometimes she says, she thinks about retiring but the money really does come in handy.

The story about Barb is very different. She was selling hot dogs out of a food cart in front of one of the big box home improvement stores. She went on to tell me that her husband lost his big paying job and was too depressed to get on with finding another job. He began to drink heavily, and gamble and she started the food cart out of necessity. Her husband has since died and at the age of 72 Barb is still working her food cart business. She owns two carts and she personally works about 2-3 days a week in one of her carts while spending other days supplying and purchasing product for her employers. She said most of the time she loves doing what she does however it is rough to work the cart over a hot grill when the temperature soars to 90 and it is hard as hell to work when the temperature drops into the teens in the winter.

I talked to one guy who recently moved to town and he told me he was looking for a job. I said, "What do you do". He said he is an eye doctor and would like to find part time work to fill the boring hours in each day. He was 77 years old.

Connie and her husband Dave retired and moved to Florida. While living in Ohio most of their lives they managed to spend a lot of their time and money at a local country club playing golf. They feel lucky to have found a similar golf club in Florida and luckier yet to have been hired to work for the club. This "high powered" business couple are now gainfully employed. Dave is a starter at the first tee on the golf course and Connie drives the beverage cart all around the course selling refreshments. Connie tells me they are living their dream - retired, making a little money and being able to play golf for free.

Did you ever notice that a lot of antique dealers are antiques themselves? Think of it this way, if you have a large collection of any kind, a basement full of dusty old books and junk that might be collectable you might be destined to start some sort of retail business with your stash of stuff, especially since you already have the initial inventory to begin with.

Carol and Paul have been collecting glassware for the past forty years. Their collection is everywhere in their house. It's in curio cabinets, on shelving and in boxes that fill up their basement and garage. They do the antique circuit and have a lot of steady customers, but they tell me that their addiction to buying far exceeds their sales. They have recently started selling on the internet through sites like eBay and Craigslist and Etsy. Occasionally they sell duplicates of their collection at a local flea market. They did tell me that each year it gets harder and harder to pack and unpack the van for shows and flea markets every weekend. Carol expressed her love and the interaction with all the friends and associates they have met over the years of doing this, so they keep on chugging along.

Knowing and talking to a lot of 70 year olds, I have come to realize there are a lot of professionals who continue to work long after retirement age.

Telephone sales has been a source of income for seniors. It is considered to be low mobility and companies allow these folks to work from home. I call it dialing for dollars. Not a bad way to earn a little money as you advance in years.

Jobs seem to be plentiful for Septuagenarians. Ted is doing senior tax returns for AARP and Joanie is giving piano lessons. Maddie is doing Bar and Bat Mitzvah tutoring and her husband Dennis is tutoring math for high school students. The AARP gig is non-paying, and the others mentioned are low-paying, however every one of them feel gratified to be doing what they are doing.

Babysitting, house sitting, and dog sitting are among other jobs being done by our 70 something crowd. You will also find them working in the grocery store, retail department stores and home improvement stores. BTW, jobs in the home improvement stores are high on the list of preferred jobs for the men in this age group. It's their way of tinkering.

Eliot was a 74-year-old who schmoozed his way into the good graces of a member of his Temple who owns a medical supply company. You guessed it, Eliot was hired to work there. He has been working there for about 5 years and just recently gave up outside sales for manning the register and greeting customers when they come in. He loves having a reason to get up and go to work four days a week and says the extra money is welcomed too. Eliot told me he would be bored silly without his job – just as long as he can have Wednesday's off for his "old codger" golf group.

While writing this book I have learned that there are a lot of professionals who continue to work long after retirement age and well into their seventies. Doctors, lawyers, CPA's, and architects are just a few professions that come to mind. There are a lot of retired individuals with advanced degrees who are well into their seventies who do consulting. I talked to Dr. Ray, a surgeon who went on to get his MBA and his law degree. At the age of 70 he has successfully combined these highly skilled professions and is now consulting with a law firm in Washington DC. He says it has almost turned out to be a full-time position based on the case he is now working on. Dr. Ray went on to tell me his "retirement profession" barely allows him time to enjoy his sailboat as often as he and his wife would like.

Working retirees is no longer an oxymoron as many "baby boomers" redefine the retirement experience. While many of them will choose to work to earn money and for the benefits, there are many other options emerging for people who want to be employed. A lot of them are reaching retirement age and choosing to continue working without missing a beat. They tell me they want to work but they want to find a way to work and have balance in their life with leisure time. Part time work is the favored work schedule.

As you have read, some of our seventy something crowd will start a new career or expand their experience into new directions. Others are looking for ways to transfer their knowledge and skill into other meaningful arenas. So, in addition to full or part time work, these Septuagenarians are evaluating their lifestyle in order to see how they can be retired and still earn income. Technology has made telecommuting the leading factor for working in the comforts of their own homes.

The concept of retirement was instituted in the mid 1930's. And, since then the nature of work as we know it has changed. It is not as physically demanding because employees have shifted from manufacturing and construction to more service and "thinking" jobs. There are lots of choices out there for all age groups.

Just to add one more thing to this discussion of Septuagenarians working into their seventies. I read on the internet that a 73-year-old woman works the midnight shift loading trucks for a company that delivers for Amazon. Another 74-year-old woman is a crossing guard and I met a 70-year-old who works at the Dollar General. Frank, at the age of 74 is still barbering and Leroy, who is 76 buys and sells junk.

The list can go on and on but one thing we know for sure, there are crazy career changes and challenges out there for seventy-year olds.

Chapter 6

# Having Fun Being Thrifty

A guy says this to his girlfriend: "I might not be rich. I have no money or villa or cars or companies like my friend John, but I love you and adore you."

She looked at me with tears in her eyes and hugged me like there is no tomorrow and whispered in my ear..." If you love me, introduce me to John..."

"Did you know that since we became seniors my husband and I do a lot of matinees?" said Rosy. She laughed and said to me, "Please get your mind out of the gutter. I am talking about movie matinees. When we do the 11:00 matinee on Wednesday's, we not only get the movie discount, we get free popcorn with our discount club card. Whoopee.

"The only problem with this movie matinee arrangement is we barely get through breakfast and here we are, at the movies eating popcorn. When we step outside after the movie we are blinded by daylight and can hardly find our parked car" said Rosy.

As I look back and think about money and fixed income and finances in general, I wish I had met John. As I was always told, it is just as easy to fall in love with a rich man as a poor man. Too bad I had to turn seventy before I realized the importance of that statement.

The more I talked to people I started to realize you don't have to be poor to try to find a bargain. In fact, some of the folks I talked to were very affluent but still loved a bargain.

Septuagenarians get a lot of discounts. When you check into a motel you can get your AARP discount even when you are not a member of AARP. They never ask to see your AARP card. I always thought AARP stood for the Advanced Aging Process. That shows you how "Arppie" oriented I am. You guessed it. I never did join that organization. Why bother?

That reminds me of another thing that I heard Septuagenarians do on a regular basis. I have interviewed a lot of couples, and they tell me they do "dunch". What, you say? You have never heard of "dunch?" Dunch is lunch and dinner combined.

There seem to be a lot of benefits for us Septuagenarians and dunch certainly is one of them. Here's what you accomplish when you do dunch. You first must check out with the restaurant what time lunch prices end. If it is three o'clock in the afternoon, then it is a perfect place to do dunch. You will get lunch time prices and be able to eat your main meal of the day at a time when you can combine lunch and dinner. Better yet, sometimes a true bargain hunter will do dunch with lunchtime prices and use a coupon to maximize on the savings.

Another couple I talked to go to Sam's club during the week just to get the oversized Nathan's hot dog combo, a hot dog

and a very large coke, for only $1.89.  Don't laugh. This is the
way a lot of seniors survive on their meager fixed incomes.
And, a very popular way to do this hot dog and oversized soft
drink is to share the drink with your spouse and buy the
combo and a single hot dog – cheaper than two combos.
That's exactly what Charlie and Penelope do when they go to
Sam's.

Some other discounts for seniors can be found in air fares, rail
passes, some restaurants, hotels and cruises.  Discounts are
everywhere for those of us that are willing to ferret them out.
We Septuagenarians seem to have the time to find them,
which is a big advantage.

Septuagenarian's also go to free concerts, and because Nancy
is an usher at the theater, she attends all the current theater in
town for free.  She says, "I merely pass out the playbill as folks
enter the theater and when the show begins, I am assigned a
seat so that I may watch the entire show free of charge.  Not a
bad gig she added.  So, ushering at the theater is usually
another way to get free tickets.

 I asked Rebecca how she managed on her Social Security
"fixed income", which was not much. She said she cuts
coupons from the paper and even tears off a coupon or two
from the magazines while in a doctor's office. She clips
coupons from the Tuesday mail package, and she reads the
sales at the grocery store meticulously. She buys BOGO's (buy
one – get one free) whenever possible. Rebecca said, even
though she lives alone, she cooks in quantity and freezes
prepared meals.  She tells me that she buys specials like
canned corn for about 44-50 cents per can and she buys about
10 at a time, cake mixes for 88 cents a box and pasta for 77

cents each. Rebecca says she buys about 10 boxes at a time. She told me she only shops at a particular store for the advertised sales.

A group of Mahjongg ladies that I spoke with go out for a bite once a week before their evening game. They share dinners at the early bird prices. So, they not only get the early bird prices, they split the bill with whoever they are sharing that dinner with. They have discovered that there are some restaurants who offer happy hour prices and those deals are even better than early bird specials. They can get appetizers during happy hour, such as a personal pizza for $5.00 or a bowl of peel and eat shrimp, for the same happy hour price.

Golfing senior discounts are another benefit made especially for 70 something's. Most golf courses give a senior discount at certain times of the day and certain days of the week. They can do this because they know the retired crowd has more free time and is not necessarily dedicated to weekend golf.

Knowing that Septuagenarians get bored I will tell you Bob and Joan's story. It is funny and well thought out. After getting up early and getting chores done, they started to realize that they got bored in the afternoon, so they began to trek on over to their favorite coffee shop for a midafternoon snack. Oh, did I tell you that Bob and Joan were a very thrifty couple and this afternoon outing started to get expensive since they were going every afternoon.

Now here's the drill. A cup of coffee was about two dollars including tax. That is four dollars for the two of them plus they add up more charges for the chocolate chip cookie, about $2.00 per cookie.

Pretty soon the coffee shop started to charge $2.02 for a cup of coffee. Joan said she never seemed to have the pennies with her, and the extra 2 cents got on her nerves. But, it was a fun outing for them each afternoon and they continued to press on with their afternoon trek to the coffee shop. She said she reached her tolerance limit when shortly after the 2 cents more per cup, they inched it up by yet one more penny. Now, a cup of coffee was costing them $2.03 per cup. It went from two dollars per cup, to $2.02 per cup, to now $2.03 per cup. Let us not forget the $2.00 each we were prone to spend at the coffee shop bakery.

Something had to give. As you know, incidents like this just remind us Septuagenarians that we are on a fixed income. Eight dollars for the pleasure of getting out of the house for an hour or so in the afternoon for a cup of coffee and a cookie was starting to play havoc on Bob and Joan's budget.

Joan laughed when she told me how they solved the financial dilemma of the afternoon coffee break. She said she bought plastic coffee mugs at the dollar store. By using their own mug, the coffee price becomes a refill price and that particular coffee shop charges only $1.26 per refill cup. That is a darn sight cheaper than the $2.03 per paper cup that they gave us at the regular purchase price Joan told me. They also realized they can go to the 7-11 store and buy three of the same size chocolate chip cookies for $1.29. Three cookies for less than one cookie at the coffee shop. So, let's do the math folks. Two coffees at $2.03 = $4.06 and two cookies at $2.00 each is another $4.00. So, they calculated they were spending $8.06 for the pleasure of an hour at the coffee shop.

The new method adds up to a great savings and they still have the pleasure of the same things. It goes like this: Two cups of coffee at the refill price in their own mugs: $1.26 x 2 = $2.52. Also, they buy three large chocolate chip cookies for a mere $1.29 at the 7-11. They take the cookies to the coffee shop in a brown paper bag. So, what used to be an $8.06 excursion every day is now an expense of $3.81 and they are getting one more cookie in the process. What a deal. Isn't it great to have that much time on your hands to learn how to be this thrifty? Leave it to the Septuagenarians to figure it out. I loved this story.

One more story on how to be thrifty. My friend Madeline invited me to do the salad bar for dinner at the Whole Foods store any time after 4:00 on Monday. Great, I said, "But why any time after 4:00 on Monday?" She told me that's when "meatless" Monday starts. You can have anything meatless in the huge salad bar, no matter what your container weighs for only $8.00. When I got there, she showed me how to pack the carry-out container so full that we were able to get enough in our containers to last for at least three days, and that is after we paid for and ate some right there on the premises.

Since most "septys" are on a fixed income, sometimes they do free lunch. Let me clue you in on free lunch. One Saturday morning my sister called and said, "What are you guys doing today"? I said we were going out to a buffet lunch. She asked me where we were going for this buffet lunch and I said, "We are going to Sam's Club".

Really, she said. I didn't know they had a buffet bar. I then told her that we go there quite often on Saturdays and eat all the samples throughout the store, and we call this our free lunch. I might add, some of the samples are much more than

44

just bite size. So, don't believe someone when they tell you there is no such thing as a free lunch. We get free lunch all the time.

Haircuts are cheaper for seniors on certain days of the week and cell phone providers are always advertising senior discounts. Some department stores offer senior discounts on certain days of the week. Oh, so many deals and not enough dollars and days to use them all.

Barbara Ann did not have much income, but she always dressed like a million bucks. I asked her what the secret to her designer wardrobe was on her fixed income. She laughed and told me she bought all of her clothes at thrift shops. The Goodwill was her Macy's and the John's Island Thrift Shoppe was her Sacks Fifth Avenue. She went on to tell me that she bought most of her jewelry at thrift shops too. Barbara Ann pointed out some of her nice pieces of furniture and accessories in her home and that they too were bought at some of the many consignment furniture stores in town. Because a lot of 70 somethings are on a fixed income, they have become very adept at finding these discounts.

Unplanned expenses, such as an appliance breaking, tend to rattle Septuagenarians because they probably have to dip into their savings accounts to pay for such items. These are times when a few seniors that I spoke to went on to tell me that they had the money to pay for things that would fall into the category of unplanned expenses. However, they realized that they did not have the ability to replace the funds being spent because they were no longer earning an income.

Even remodeling, when necessary or desired, can be done in a thrifty way. Nancy told me her son taught her this one. A few years ago, she bought countertops at Lowe's and asked them if she could use Lowe's coupons to pay for them. They said yes, she could, Nancy said she went to the grocery store and bought gift cards to use at the home improvement store. The points she received at the grocery store from spending the money on the gift card enabled her to get a large discount on her gas at their pumps. Nancy went on to tell me that there are many gift cards you can buy at her local supermarket in order to get her gas discounts.

Oh, by the way, she also told me that when she bought the counter tops and the new appliance for her kitchen remodel she was also able to take advantage of the one year – no finance charge that the home improvement store was offering.

When you are out shopping and saving money there is one more thing I want to mention. You might plan your shopping excursion with an "app" dinner. Wow, what is an "app" dinner you might ask? There are many restaurants that have bars that feature a happy hour with appetizers. The drinks are usually half price or two for one and the "app" menu usually features appetizers for about $5.00. My friend and I go to a very upscale place and do wine and "apps". She ordered the sliders and I got a bowl of steamed mussels and we shared an additional appetizer of shrimp. All that food for only $7.50 per person. And, it was delicious.

Another way to be thrifty is to make sure your doctors are prescribing generic drugs when possible. They are a lot cheaper than non-generics.

As you can see, being thrifty can be fun and beneficial. You just have to plan ahead a little and the savings make it all worthwhile.

# Chapter 7

# Septuagenarians
# Are Parents Too

Two kids are talking to each other. One says, "I'm really worried. My dad works twelve hours a day to give me a nice home and good food. My mom spends the whole day cleaning and cooking for me. I'm worried sick!"

The other kid says, "What have you got to worry about? Sounds to me like you've got it made."

The first kid says, "What if they try to escape?"

Did you know that becoming a gardener requires more preparation than parenting? And, did you know, parenting does not get any easier when you become a Septuagenarian?

We bring up our kids so they do not need us and then all of a sudden we are in our 70s and that is when we realize we need them.

By the time I hit my seventies I learned everything wrong with my kids, in their minds, was the fault of my parenting. At the same time, I sometimes think everything wrong with me is the result of my parenting. Hmmm. After interviewing on this subject, I do not stand alone with regard to this feeling.

I talked to Barbara and she put it this way. "I just wish my kids had taken the time to ask me questions about me. It seemed as though it was always about them."

There is nothing worse than turning 70 and trying to save for your old age only to find out that what little savings you have are being squandered by a child. That is what is happening to Edie. She went on to tell me that she took a chunk of her savings to lend her son money to buy a little business and he promised to pay her back. At the beginning she met up with him once a week and he began to pay her back, but as time went on and the business was not as successful as he assumed it would be, she was not getting paid back. Not only was she not getting paid back, her son keeps borrowing just a little more each month to float his business or his lifestyle it seems. He seems to have money to travel and buy his male toys but never seems to have the money to pay his mother back. Edie says, she is caught between a rock and a hard place in their relationship.

So, when you become a parent, no matter your age, it becomes a way of life all the rest of the days of your life.  Usually by the time you are a Septuagenarian your children are grown and usually have children of their own and that is their focus, not you, unless you are called upon to baby sit their children or their children's children. By the time you reach your mid to late 70s you are not necessarily up to taking care of a great grandchild. It would probably interfere with your nap time.

Joanne said that those big Thanksgiving dinners she used to spend weeks preparing now become a lonely Holiday. Joanne and her husband moved to Florida and it didn't take them long to realize their children would not be spending too many holidays with them. Her son and his wife usually spend the Holiday with his in-laws and her daughter's family goes to a ski resort every Thanksgiving. What does all of this mean? It means a lonely Holiday for Mom and Dad. That's what it means.

Another Septuagenarian Mom whom I interviewed tells me her children always phone on the Holiday, however, that does not alleviate the loneliness of not being with them. Being excluded from most of the big holidays because their children are not able or willing to make it for a visit still hurts she said – even though she has offered to pay plane fare. She went on to say that she usually spends holidays with a friend of hers who is in the same boat. Instead of cooking that big holiday meal, she said, they usually go to a restaurant.  This feeling of loneliness was shared over and over again by long distance parents.

I talked to Linda at length and she says it was a rude awakening for her to realize that once a son gets married, they fall into step with their wives' families. She has two sons, both living in upstate NY and her sons barely talk to one another let alone spend holidays with her and her husband. At the early stages of her son's marriages it soon became the norm for her sons to NOT spend holidays with them. Linda realized parenting is different at this age because there is another family involved.

I was able to interview a lot of 70-year olds who lived in Florida and the lack of involvement with their grown children seemed to be one of their biggest complaints. They talked about how they did not miss the snow, but they missed family holiday dinners with their kids. I also spoke with Floridian's who have made the trek back North often to be with their families at these special times.

Mary Beth, who spent six months in Florida and six months up North had a sad story to tell. She had three children, twin girls and one son. Her twin daughters were estranged from one another and the son was not on speaking terms with his dad. All three of the siblings lived about 100 miles in different directions of each other. She and her husband actually flew to NY for Thanksgiving and Christmas and Mary Beth would spend the holiday with her son and his children while her husband Mike divided his time between the daughters. She said it always made holidays complicated and very stressful.

The "holiday sharing pattern" usually starts early in their children's marriages and becomes more noticeable when you reach your seventies. Seems like in the beginning, they do seem to be able to share the holidays between families, but the sharing becomes less and less as the years go by and by the time you are a Septuagenarian it becomes a sad day when you realize that you are no longer seeing your children on these special days.

Diane and Henry were pioneers when it came to sharing holidays. She and her husband had nothing in common with their daughter-in-law's family however she never wanted to lose her newly married son to the usual holiday split, so she started off their very first Thanksgiving holiday by inviting her daughter-in-law's family to join in. It's been the same every major holiday since then and everyone gets to be together as family.

Given the way the world is, things are more complicated regarding parenting than ever before. I will give you an example. I talked to Fred and he tells me that his step daughter was planning her wedding. Her parents were divorced and the groom's parents were divorced, and her grandparents were divorced. It made for a very interesting array of parents and grandparents for this couple and certainly did complicate the wedding.

Do they go to her mother's or her father's home for the holidays because they both have significant others or do they go to his mother's or his father's or do they go to her grandmother's or her grandfather's or do they go to his grandparents'? If your children are from a broken home or have married into a broken home this dilemma is a natural outcome. It makes it all the more difficult for 70-year olds to dream of a real "Holiday" with their children. That is what I am hearing over and over again.

One last thing about holidays such as Christmas and Thanksgiving. I've heard a lot about how some children attend the holiday dinner between both sets of parents. Rebecca tells me that she has to plan her Thanksgiving feast to be eaten at a late dinner hour because her two kids and their family's go to their in-laws for an early dinner. Of course, she has cooked the meal for days and the kids are still sated from the early dinner so they do not eat much. She told me she has solved that problem by having take-home containers and fills them up with "meals to go". In this manner there are no gastric disasters from overeating.

I hear from some of these 70-year olds that their children still seem to blame their parents for any and all of their woes. One such parent told me she thinks it's because it's her adult child's way of dodging responsibility. You know, blame the parents for everything. Hmmm.

Between the holiday complications and adult children blaming their parents for everything it does not surprise me to hear that a lot of Septuagenarians have settled in to making their own lives matter, especially around the holidays. They have learned how to enjoy the phone calls from their children and not to expect too much more from them.

Becca tells me she enjoys lunch with her son about once a week and Joan says she enjoys an early dinner with her dad at a restaurant a few times a month. During several of my interviews I did ask a question regarding lunch or dinners out with their grown children. I asked who pays. People were all over the board with their answers however I did begin to see a pattern. The sons usually picked up the tab for their Mothers and the Dads usually paid for their daughters.

Of course, finances do play a big part when it comes to relationships between children and their Septuagenarian parents. Discussions about money and parenting are all over the map. Sometimes the kids have more money than the parents and sometimes the parents have more than the kids. Well, that makes sense, doesn't it?

Take Toni for example. She did not have a lot of money, but she had managed to save up some money for her old age as she put it. Her son Jack made a good living however he went through a divorce and his ex-wife got the house and some cash – no children involved in their short marriage. After the divorce Jack asked his mother to lend him $10,000.00 so that he could buy another house for himself. He assured her that he would pay her back. Since Toni was a sucker for her son, him being the baby and the only boy, she lent him the money.

Her son was a fireman who had another business on the side so Toni always assumed he would pay her back. A few years went by and he did not make any effort to pay his mother back. Then one day, she tells me, her hot water tank went out. Since she was not necessarily rolling in dough as she says, she asked her son to take care of the hot water tank since she lent him $10,000.00. Toni told me he got furious with her for asking him to pay for a hot water tank because she lent him money. He did not see any connection between the two issues. He was angry with her for mentioning to her daughter that she had the nerve to ask him to pay for the water heater. She stews over the $10,000.00 which she lent her son and now Toni is on the outs with her son because she asked him to pay for the hot water tank.

These kind of money issues with grown children are not necessarily a rare issue. Rebecca lent her son money to play poker in a tournament while his wife and children were visiting her family in Florida.

Like Toni, Rebecca could not afford to carelessly lend her son money, but she did so because he asked, and she too assumed he would pay her back. Needless to say, he did not win the poker tournament and she never saw the money. Why do kids ask their parents for a loan if they never have any intentions of paying it back? Just asking.

When asking the question, "Have you ever had to lend your grown children money" to Betty Ann, I got an unusual answer. She went on to tell me that on one occasion she had a dire need to borrow money from her son and she promised to pay it back at the first opportunity she could. Her son, who had the money did reluctantly lend her $5,000.00 and she went on to tell me she paid him back in just a few short months. You would think that was a "good son" gesture, however Betty Ann went on to tell me that for years to come he has always brought up the fact that she had to borrow money from him. Apparently, the children do not like to think of a parent needing to borrow from them, even when they have more than the parent.

The more I talked to these 70 somethings about parenting, the more I was hearing that they did not necessarily have problems with their children, but the spouses of their children are where they seemed to be having the most problems. The evil daughter-in-law or the ne'er do well son-in-law were the subject of discontent among many whom I interviewed.

Take Diane for instance. Her son is trapped in an unhappy marriage with an evil wife. Now I have heard a lot of stories about those evil daughters-in-law however Diane's story tops them all. Things were OK but not real warm and fuzzy for the longest time until she was hit with the awful news that her son had cancer. Diane said she thought perhaps her daughter-in-law would show compassion and be a little less hard on her and her son, especially since they had a three-year-old and twins on the way. Diane went on to say that her daughter-in-law was not able to take her husband for chemo because of the pregnancy so Diane was more than willing to do the chemo thing with her son.

She remembers taking her son to his first chemo treatment. Diane picked him up in the morning from his house after his recent surgery and on the way out of the house, his evil wife hollered out to him, "Don't forget to pick up a quart of milk on your way home."

Diane went on to tell me that "shout out" for milk set the pace for the next three years during Bradley's chemo's and further surgeries. Brad's wife almost never gave Diane access to her grandson and she remained cold and uncaring regarding her husband's cancer throughout the ordeal. Diane had to come to the realization that her son was stuck in an unhappy marriage with the "evil" daughter-in-law. She ended the conversation with this. "It is what it is".

Another "evil" daughter-in-law story came from Marilyn. Her son's wife was attached to the hip with her family. They lived within blocks of each other and were always in and out of each other's homes. Marilyn, who lived at the other end of town, saw little of her grandson and frankly stopped buying toys that were mounting up at her house. She recalled on her grandson's fifth birthday Tony insisted his wife invite his parents to the 5th birthday party. The daughter-in law had a big theme-oriented party for the birthday boy with her entire family invited to the all-day party – a cookout and cake and ice cream, games for the kids and tons of presents and then when the party ended, she reluctantly invited Anthony's family to come for cupcakes at 7:00 in the evening. When Tony's family arrived at 7:00 they pulled into the driveway and Ms. Evil ran out to tell them hey, you will have to park on the street so the last of her relatives could leave the driveway. How disappointing that his family were not included in the "real" birthday party as they viewed her family leaving.

Daughters-in-law, sons-in-law, and everything in between is always a topic for discussion however, I think I will leave that alone other than what I have already said.

The one thing I learned after talking to many 70-year-old parents is that blood is thicker than water. Ask any parent who has married children. Seems as though, in most cases, the in-laws never seem to quite live up to a parent's expectations.

One parent I talked to told me that she used to have issues with her son and every time she tried to talk to him on the phone about something that was bothering her, he pooh poohed the conversation with a very simple sentence. "Oh mom", he said, "Let it go". It didn't matter what she said after that, he just said let it go. Maybe we should let it go and stop parenting and just enjoy... but as I said in the beginning of this chapter, parenting is a lifelong job and it seems to be nearly impossible to just "let it go".

I talked to a few children who had 70-year-old parents regarding their relationships with their parents and the stories were all over the place. The one thing I did recognize was that 70 something's with daughters seemed to have a more comfortable relationship than Septuagenarians with sons. That discussion would take up too much of our time to go into this observation of mine.

One thing I have learned after interviewing a lot of folks about parenting is the fact that you cannot escape from this job, no matter your age. You were never taught that the hardest part of parenthood is when your kids grow up. When they are young they need you and it seems when they grow up they spend their adult years trying not to need you. The problem with that is you begin to realize you need them.

James told me the thing that seems to bother him most as a 70 something parent is the fact that his sons are now telling him what to do instead of him telling them what to do.

"One fabulous part of parenting at this age is grand parenting" said Linda. And being a great grandparent is a real bonus. This makes it all worthwhile say most all of the grandparents I have interviewed.

.

# Chapter 8

# The Spiritual Scene

One night a lady came home from her weekly prayer meeting, found she was being robbed, and she shouted out, "Acts 2:38: 'Repent and be baptized and your sins will be forgiven.' The robber quickly gave up and the lady rang the police. While handcuffing the criminal, a policeman said, "Gee mate, you gave up pretty easily. How come you gave up so quickly?" The robber said, "She said she had an axe and two 38's!"

When talking to Septuagenarians about their faith I got the sense they did not have much humor on the subject of religion. For a lot of them, they went to their place of worship on a regular basis more for the social aspect and not necessarily to speak to God. For some, they observed religious services to ease their loneliness.

Marilyn said she loved the first Friday night service at her Temple. At this service the Rabbi calls up all members who are celebrating their birthdays and they sing happy birthday in English and Hebrew and knowing that they cannot call out a specific person's name the Rabbi always sings happy birthday to "these Jews". I always get a chuckle out of this. "Of course, there is a box brought out after the singing for the children of all ages, even 70-year olds, to select a little toy" said Marilyn.

Attending a service or mass gives our 70s crowd a reason to dress up and be out among like-minded people. It gives them a sense of community when they are among their "Church friends".

While talking to them about religion, I noticed that the answers were all over the place. One question was – what religion if any do you practice, and if you practice, how often do you go to your Church or Synagogue?

I learned Septuagenarians were somewhat obsessed with end of life issues. That seemed to be one reason a lot of 70 somethings attended their Church or Temple on a regular basis. Being involved gave them a sense of peace knowing they would have a more personal end of life experience (a funeral) if they were a member of a Church or Synagogue.

A lot of the answers I got were way out there and a lot of the responses were easy to understand but I was seeing in my interviews that 70-year olds most often considered some form of religion in their lives to be of importance and a lot of them observe on a regular basis.

I had a chuckle when I got to the question of what religion do you practice? Does that mean they are practicing so that they get better at religion or are they practicing because they are rusty and need more practice, or is it a game and they need to practice more often to get better at the game? Oh well, just thinking. I wonder why I did not just ask "what is your religion" instead of "what religion do you practice"?

Sandy told me that she and her husband go to Synagogue every Friday night because they enjoy and need the sense of community they get from attending on a regular basis. They know most everyone in the congregation and after services there is a social gathering of the attendees called the Oneg Shabbat. It's almost like going to a party every Friday night she said.

The UU (Universalist Unitarian) Church does the same after their services I am told. Karen says the best part of the service at the UU is the coffee hour immediately following the service.

Karen and her husband Fred made their way to the UU when they reached their mid-seventies after a long and winding road. She considered herself to be a Christian but did not go to any Church for many years until they started attending the UU.

How they found their way to the UU was an interesting story. Karen told me Fred was brought up Jewish and after he married his first wife, who was not Jewish, he more or less gave up on religion. When he went to Church with her, which he often did, he told the minister, "Do NOT try to convert me because it is not going to happen". Years later, after two divorces, Fred and Karen married. Religion was not an issue with them. They did not go to Church and by this time Fred was not interested in religion of any kind. It was not until they were in their mid-70s they joined the Unitarian Universalist Church.

Karen went on to tell me of their journey. Interestingly enough, joining in for services at the UU never did have anything to do with God she said. They went to the UU which was conveniently located right across the street from their house for several events such as a concert, or a book signing, or an interesting lecture series given at the Church. Soon they started going to the Church Services on Sunday's because it seemed like the right thing to do and she tells me the same thing that Sandy was telling me. They enjoyed the coffee hour after the service in the same way that Sandy and her husband enjoyed the Oneg Shabbat at the Jewish congregation.

I found this to be a common thread with the Septuagenarian's that I talked to on this subject of religion. They became affiliated, not because of a deep need to find or be with God but a need to involve themselves in the social aspect of belonging to a congregation. Karen told me she attends the women's lunches while Fred goes to some of the men's functions. Karen also became a member of the choir and looks forward to choir practice. Karen went on to tell me that she never had children and never had the pull to belong to any Church until she became an active member of the UU. She went on to tell me that because of her affiliation with the UU she would probably never move too far away from this congregation. Now that she is in her seventies, she realizes that she is fulfilling needs with this Church that she never again would want to be without. Her sense of community with the friends she and Fred have made through the Church is what makes them happy to have joined.

Lynette and Craig, practicing Catholic's, went to the Saturday mass instead of Sunday mass because it was much more convenient for them. In fact, going to mass became part of their Saturday night date. They went to mass and after mass they then got on with their evening. In other words, the Catholic mass only – no hanging around afterwards for social and refreshments. How different that was from the Jewish Oneg Shabbat and the social hour after the service at the UU.

Lynette went on to tell me that she and Craig, both of them were considered to be sexy 70s, had started to talk about the possibility of marriage. Since they were Catholic you would think that was not going to be a problem. But, since her first marriage ended in divorce and, unless her first husband were dead, she was not free to remarry in the Catholic Church said her priest because the first marriage was not annulled. Hmmm.

George and Carol went to mass every Sunday morning and then met up with a couple who were lifelong friends for breakfast after mass. George was always a bit late for breakfast because he was an usher at the 9:00 mass. Sounds to me as though they created their own "coffee hour" after Church.

I talked to one gal who went to Church every Sunday morning at one of those outdoor services. There were hundreds attending every Sunday and she also became involved in some Church activities during the week. It was a matter of getting and staying involved that kept her interested in that congregation. She went on to tell me that she has met a few members and on occasion they go to breakfast after Sunday services. Again, the reoccurring social aspect of attending on a regular basis and chatting up with a few people after services was the reason a lot of 70 somethings attended on a regular basis.

One woman I talked to who will remain anonymous, told me that she loves to shop, and she goes to her Temple on a regular basis just so that she could use her very "stylish" wardrobe. I laughed at that one.

I asked this question of most of the people I interviewed with regards to their religion. "Do you feel God's presence while in a house of God?"

Seems as though very few folks I talked to, who attended any kind of an organized and recognized religion, mentioned God. Even when I asked the question outright – do you feel a relationship with God when you are in Church or Temple, or Synagogue? I could not get an answer. Some felt a sense of peace, some felt happy to be worshiping, some felt good about going to their place of worship on a regular basis but, hardly any, when pushed to answer that question said they felt God while "in" a house of God. In fact, a lot of them said they felt the need to feel God while attending religious mass or services and wondered about the absence. Hmmm.

I was getting similar answers to this question until I talked with Janette. When I asked her what, if any Church she attended Janette told me she attended an Old Catholic Church where the mass was still held in Latin and that is the way she liked it to be. "Yes", she said. I feel God's presence when in Church and I need his presence. She went on to say there have been tragedies in her life including the loss of two sons. She did not necessarily turn to the Church for solace however while attending mass she always felt God's presence. I asked her why she didn't turn away from God because of her losses – you know, like saying, "Why God? If you are a real God, why would you take both of my sons?" Janette told me she came to realize that without his presence she would not have been able to cope with her loses.

Dorothy, a 76-year-old Catholic woman that I interviewed told me she goes to Church every Saturday to the 4:00 mass and to this very day she rarely eats meat on Fridays. No more getting up early on a Sunday for mass since they started having mass on Saturdays and Sundays. She said knowing that she is not obligated to Sundays only and knowing that she can now eat meat on Fridays has made keeping her faith easier as she has aged.

I personally can identify with Dorothy about letting go of old customs. As a child, my parents attended an Orthodox Synagogue where the women actually sat upstairs behind a curtain during the service. Wow, I thought…. this is definitely not for me. I did not know any better at the time. It was such a turnoff that I did not get involved until I had my first child. At that time, I did not hesitate but to join a reformed Temple, a place where Judaism could be practiced by men and women on an equal basis and where the services were held in English and Hebrew.

Ruth Ann said she has been Jewish all her life. She said, I can honestly say at this juncture I don't give much thought to the religious aspect of my life.  I believe in God, and I try to live my life according to the ten commandants. Ruth Ann went on to say "It is that simple - it is what it is, and I am what I am – by birth and by choice and I have learned not to dwell on it, nor do I wear my religion on my sleeve."

Ruth Ann's thoughts were very similar to most people I talked to. Seems they just took their particular religion for granted and had no desire to reach out and learn about other choices. Some were converts to a particular religion thru marriage, some by choice but most everyone I talked to stuck to the same faith as the one they were brought up in.

I interviewed Bena who told me she dabbles in Kabbalah
hoping to find a deeper meaning to her Judaism. What is
Kabbalah? The word Kabbalah means "receiving." It's the
study of how to receive fulfillment in your life and Jew's are
not the only ones who are embracing Kabbalah. Madonna is a
good example of a person not of the Jewish faith who
considers herself a Kabbalist. Other noted people who study
Kabbalah are Britney Spears, Roseanne Barr, Ashton Kutcher,
Demi Moore, Mick Jagger, Donna Karan and Paris Hilton.

I got the impression that people I was talking to involve
themselves in their Church or Synagogue for the very same
reason – to receive fulfillment in their lives.

Septuagenarians are more apt to participate in religious
services in the traditional way than younger individuals.
There are various times for services from Friday night through
Sunday, depending on your religious affiliation. It is often the
highlight of their week and they tell me they love going for
the interaction with other like individuals. They say they get a
sense of community when they attend.

A large percentage of those I talked to consider themselves
spiritual while a very small percentage are atheists, in other
words they do not seek meaningfulness in their lives through
religion or a spiritual life.

Since most of the Septuagenarians I talked to say religion
plays a major role in their lives, they say they are bothered by
the fact they cannot seem to keep their children or their
grandchildren interested enough to attend the rituals of
religious services. Maddie seemed to think part of the reason
for this might be because she cannot imagine her grandson

parting with his cell phone long enough to sit through a
service. Hmmm.

Some of the folks I interviewed tell me they chose not to
belong because they could not afford to pay the yearly dues.
Some religions seem to come with a price tag and I am hearing
this from more than one or two people interviewed. One
person I talked to who shall remain anonymous told me that
she talked to the Rabbi and they created a special reduced fee
for her - something she could afford to pay from her fixed
income. Another person interviewed told me that she can
afford to pay her yearly dues however, her married children
could not. Not a good way for the expression – *the family that
prays together stays together* I concluded.

The Spiritual Scene

Chapter 9

# Dating During Your 70's

*Remember when you used to be able to call a person 57 times, and hang up, and they never knew it was you.*

I would give him an organ, but never will I marry him" said Susan. Susan dated on line for the better part of seven years and then she met and fell in love with Jim. She made it very clear as the relationship developed into a romance that she had no intentions of re-marrying. I hear that a lot from many of the dating 70-year olds.

Women I interviewed tell me men they meet are either boring, bald or big bellied and the nice looking ones want a younger woman. Some of the men I have talked to about dating would rather be golfing, fishing, or bowling than to take the time to meet a woman. And, men who are involved in a relationship seem to put golfing, fishing, and bowling first while what his gal friend is cooking for dinner seems to be what he likes best about her. Women... be wary of the men who are looking for a nurse and a purse.

Widowers (men) have a tendency to get "fixed up" more than women do, and they usually fall in love soon after meeting a gal. And, since there are somewhere close to 5 single

Septuagenarian women to every single man in their seventies well... you get the picture.

What does a Septuagenarian woman want in a relationship? Most of the women I have talked to want pretty much the same thing. Companionship and friendship float to the top of their list. They seem to want someone to share conversation with and someone whom they can enjoy an evening out with – be it a movie, dinner in a nice restaurant, the theater or a sporting event.

Septuagenarian dating is as exciting and as volatile as dating at any age. When exchanging phone numbers, you wait by the phone wondering if he or she will call and if you get "the" call what will you say or talk about. What seems to work best for most of my friends who got "the call" was to do a meet up for a cup of coffee to see if they are compatible. That meet up can pretty much be summed up as a first date.

One woman whom I shall call Annette has admitted to meeting men and she says she is not capable of recognizing the signs of interest fast enough to act upon them. She said she started to chat with a guy during one of her exercise classes, found out he was recently widowed, if two years can be considered recent, and found him nice to look at. The class was on a Monday and she said he always greeted her with a smile and asked how her weekend was. One Monday he even went so far as to put his arm around her shoulder and say, "how's my girlfriend?" Annette said she knew if she would just give him a nudge, he very well might want to actually consider asking her out on a date. But something didn't seem right to Annette. The more Annette and I talked the more she was able to tell me the "not so right" part about Gary. She said he talked about his deceased wife all the time and he still wore his wedding ring. She said one time they were talking about cooking for one and Gary said he ate at his daughter's house every night because she lived right across the street from him. Hmmm. That would be a cause for concern for me too if I met a guy with all those red flags.

Another Septuagenarian I spoke with told me her "dating" story. Apparently, she had a steady telephone boyfriend. They went out a few times and soon he was calling her every day- sometimes even more than once a day and pretty much kept her on a short leash with promises of seeing her and dating her more often, however the physical appearance of Doug just did not happen as frequently as she had hoped. Brenda said she came to realize it was not much of a relationship that she and Doug had but she still looked forward to his calls every day. She said no one else, not even her son, showed as much concern for her as did Doug so she continued her phone relationship - love affair.

Another on-line dating story had a happy ending...or so I thought. Rachel and Bob began spending a lot of time together and soon the romance blossomed. They were together all the time, pictures of lovey-dovey stuff on Facebook was seen by everyone and maybe a year passed and all of a sudden no more pictures of Rachel and Bob were appearing on FB. Soon it was obvious there was someone else in her life. Her new love was another one of her on-line meet-ups. I never got the whole story from Rachel, but it seems to me that her on-line search never ended even while dating Bob until she found someone that she liked more. So, would you consider Rachel having a happy ending or is she just an opportunist who is always looking for the greenest grass? Just asking...

One of the pitfalls for a lot of 70-year-old women regarding dating seems to be a lack of men. And that leads me to the next interview with Marci. Marci took up with a married man and has been seeing him for the past four years. During the first three years they saw each other on a regular basis, and she fell deeply in love with her married lover. As you may have guessed, it started to bother her that she spent weekends and holidays alone while he continued to live with his wife and family. She did not tell me that she pressured him to leave his wife, but she made it obvious to me in the interview that the fact he was married was beginning to take its toll on the relationship. He was seeing her less and less which bothered her more and more until it became very obvious that the relationship was doomed. To this very day, she clings to the crumbs he now gives her which is nowhere near the attention and time she got from him during the first three years. I guess the moral of this story is no different than what happens to women at any age – do not date a married man.

Not all dating situations with a married man are failures. I interviewed a 72-year-old woman who was seeing a married man with a much different story. His wife had Alzheimer's and barely knew who he was. George was an honorable and devoted husband who went to visit his wife every day in the memory care unit and then, with little or no guilt, he saw Laura. After visiting with his wife every day, he then devoted the remainder of his time and thoughts towards Laura. He showered Laura with attention – phone calls and dinners and lunches, flowers on special occasions and gifts. Laura, who just got out of a mentally abusive 50-year marriage, enjoyed his company and the attention he gave her. She was not at all bothered by his affection and devotion to his wife of many years. She had no intention of ever getting married again so this arrangement with a married man worked fine for her.

A lot of the men and women I have talked with about dating tell me that they have pretty much given up on the whole thing. "A short stint on one of the senior on-line dating sites left me a bit uneasy" said Annie. I got a couple of flirts, and one almost date the first week on the site and not much more after that. Annie said she wrote on her profile that she would only be interested in men who lived within a fifty-mile radius. Pretty soon she was getting flirts and messages from men all over the country. She went on to say it became important to recognize the scammers who preyed on older women on these dating sites. Annie said she Googled on-line scamming on dating sites and learned how to recognize the "red flags".

Annie told me she met one guy on line who she clicked with – they had a lot in common and talked for the better part of an hour on their first coffee meet up. When the conversation started to lag, she said she thought it was time to end the first meet up, so she made moves to put on her coat and they soon walked out to their cars. What was she was supposed to do at this point, she told me. Was she supposed to say thank you for the cup of coffee, it was nice meeting you, or should she say I had a great time with you today and I hope we can do this again, or was she just supposed to get in her car and say goodbye? Since this was Annie's first meet up she said shaking hands did not seem appropriate so, as an instinct she said very casually to her coffee first date "give me a hug". Annie told me she hugged him at the car door and noticed he recoiled a bit so…. that was the end of her casual goodbye. She went on to tell me that after a few days went by she was still thinking of him in a nice sort of way that she decided to text him and thank him for the meet up and tell him how well she thought their first meet up went. She told him she had a family vacation planned in Florida for the next 10 days, and she hinted that she had hoped to see him again when she returned. He texted her back with a yes, indeed, they seemed to have a lot in common. He even went so far as to tell her in that text that he felt he already knew her. Annie showed me the text messages leading up to the first date and the rest of the messages and it definitely led her to believe they would see each other again.

When she got back from her vacation and after a few days had passed with no word from him she sent him a text stating that she was back in town and tanned and rested – with her second hint that she would like to see him again. Here is the answer she got. "Great" he said in the text....and not another word was ever heard from this guy again.

Annie told me this story in its entirety because she wanted me to know that this whole on-line dating scene really turned her off. She said she would much rather meet guys and flirt with them in person and never again will she put so much emphasis on that cup of coffee meet up. She said she also came to the conclusion that guys will meet up with a lot of women from these dating sites and do so while still being involved with another. Sneaking out to a faraway place for a cup of coffee with a meet up sort of a date would be a little like cheating on your wife or girlfriend. Just saying.

I checked on line and found out that Silver Singles, Match.com and Our Time are among the top ten senior dating sites. Since I was having a difficult time interviewing men while writing this book I finally caved in and joined an on-line dating service in order to get male input towards the end of the book. Mission accomplished. I was reading so many male profiles and getting flirts from guys and even on occasion a few conversations that I found myself immersed into a new thing. For the first week or so I spent a lot of time at my message board and only had one conversation.  Since I was in unchartered territory I was cautioned that women our age are prey for a lot of scammers. So, I warn all of you women who are into this mode of meeting men to be very careful. I'm going to leave it at that. And, I always had Annie's story about her experience with her coffee date in the back of my mind.

I got bored with spending my time perusing the message boards and looking to see who was flirting with me that I started to delete my e-mails every day but kept the sight open since I paid for this privilege. But, in all fairness to on-line dating, it still beats sitting in a bar and drinking and hoping someone will pay attention to you. Also, from what a lot of people have told me, the bar scene is pretty much a dead-end road for seniors. Just saying.

Linda fought all the obstacles and plodded on with the on-line dating.  She was serious about finding a boyfriend and found these sites to be her method of finding love. Or so she thought. Seems like every guy she met from her on-line venture was either cheap, he lived too far, or they just didn't have any chemistry.  She said when she would meet someone that she thought she might like to continue seeing she realized that after two or three dates she was able to recognize the signs that he was just not into her.

I was lucky enough to get one man's point of view on internet dating and it goes like this. Dale lived in a small town in Ohio and after his divorce, he knew he did not want anyone to know what he was doing so he lied on his profile that he was posting on a senior dating site. He said he lived in FL. when in fact he was living in Ohio. Since Dale was a man of means he did not fear the expense of flying to FL. to meet women if he were lucky enough to connect with one. He proceeded to text, e-mail and talk by phone for about a month with a particular woman and concluded that he did indeed want to spend time and get to know her. By this time, they had conversed enough to not just make it a cup of coffee somewhere. Dale made arrangements to spend a week together at her place in Florida. Now my readers, don't get your hopes up for a happy ever after ending to this story. Dale went on to tell me this encounter was the week from hell. He said she criticized him…. he was driving too slowly, he was driving too fast and she carped on him on everything in between. He said one week with her sent him flying back to Ohio real fast.

One very big advantage of dating on-line is that you can do it from the comfort of your home. You don't have to depend on your married friends fixing you up with one of their unmarried friends and you don't have to go to the bars hoping to meet up with someone.

Sometimes 70-year olds who date really do lead to "happily ever after". Take Lynn and Frank for example. They met, they dated, they fell in love, they got engaged and that is as far as they got. Once they started to try to come to grips with tying the knot they ran into a snag. Frank would have to leave his home which was on the opposite end of town to move into Lynn's large, three story condo where life would be better for them. Apparently, Lynn confessed, his house was now and forever going to be the home where the grown children revered their deceased mother and it was never going to be comfortable for her. And, his 45-year-old son had the basement apartment and all five of his siblings were in and out of the house at all hours. Lynn and Frank got over all the hurdles of dating, falling in love, and deciding they wanted to get married and spend their twilight years cozy as two lovebirds in her condo when the other shoe dropped. Hmmm. Only one car garage and a very lousy parking situation at the condo has put a stop to the whole living "happily ever after". They are actually fighting over who will get the garage. Boy, this one is a toughie.

I guess the moral of this story about dating while in your seventies is that anything goes. There seems to be no right or wrong – just whatever works for you is what you should do. Let's face it, the chance of meeting your soulmate at this stage and age are about nil.

Chapter 10
# The Sexy 70's

An elderly couple had been dating for some time and decided it was finally time to marry. Before the wedding, they had a long conversation regarding how their marriage might work. They discussed finances, living arrangements and so on.

Finally, the old man decided it was time to broach the subject of their physical relationship. "How do you feel about sex?" he asked, rather hopefully.

"Well, I'd like to say I like it infrequently," she responded.

The old guy paused, then he asked, "Was that one word or two?"

Some say that when it comes to sex, the seventies are like the new twenties. I wouldn't go that far but I can tell you what I am hearing from some of my interviews, it certainly might be reminiscent of their forties.

Rolling Stones front man, Sir Mick Jagger, has become a father again at the age of 73. I rest my case.... there is sex in the lives of Septuagenarians. This chapter will deal with sex as we call it during your Septuagenarian years. While interviewing women who had boyfriends and men who had girlfriends, I began to realize that there are a lot of active Septuagenarians. Just ask any senior who lives in "the Villages", a large retirement community in Central Florida.

While having a profound interest in sexual pleasure, 70-year olds still fear getting STD's – Sexual Transmitted Diseases. As a matter of precaution, when you are on the brink of a sexual relationship with a new partner, it would be wise to have yourself tested for everything related to STD's, especially if living in The Villages in Florida or any retirement community in Palm Springs, CA. Both locations are mecca's for sexually active seniors, therefore they are communities that are susceptible to STD's.

Sleepovers that might include sex for Septuagenarians have their share of problems however, it might not be what you would expect. Take Madeline for example. A bunch of her friends got together for a Christmas party. Madeline was really into her beau, so she invited him to go to the party and then spend the night. Madeline's guy Craig who lived on the other side of town was a super nice guy and she wanted to show him off to her friends. He adored Madeline and liked to call her his "arm candy". As the story of this particular night goes, Madeline's daughter works for a men's clothing store and Madeline, since she was excited to show off her guy at the Christmas party, she gave him his Christmas presents early - new gentleman's attire that she picked out for him at her daughter's place of employment. She really wanted him to look nice so she could show him off to her friends.

By the way, speaking of men's clothing, if I ever met a guy wearing a leisure suit I would run just as fast as I could away from him. That is almost as bad as black knee socks with Bermuda shorts or long bushy sideburns.

Getting back to Madeline and Craig's sleepover. Madeline rode to the party with one of her friends. Craig met up with her a little later in the evening because he went to Church prior to the party/dinner dance. Since this was a senior function the doors opened at 4:30 which is about par for the course for this age group. The evening opened up with a very crowded dance floor of line dancers.  They were really into it, especially since partners are not required for this type of dancing so…. yes, as always, there were a lot more women out on the dance floor than there were men.

A good time was had by all during the evening and as planned, Craig was going to be the one to take Madeline home since they had staked out their sleepover.

They arrived back to her place at about 9:30 which was a late night out for them. Now, here's the funny part, in spite of the best laid plans for spending the night with her new boyfriend, when they got back to her house, he realized he could not spend the night with her because he forgot his insulin. With a moan and a groan, after dropping her off, he had to back off from the sleepover and make the long drive home to the other end of town at that late hour. Moral of this story is…when you are in your 70s, don't forget your meds when you plan a sleepover.

There are a lot of pitfalls to planning a sleepover with your new found romance other than forgetting to pack your meds.

I talked to another gal who told me she was afraid of a sleepover because she suffered incontinence.  She said it would embarrass her to death if she had to be caught wearing her adult diaper panties. Just saying.

Another interview I had with Mary, a 74-year-old, petite redhead, told me the most annoying problem she and her boyfriend had when he spends the night is his snoring. She said it is so loud that he might just peel the paint off the wall, so she usually ends up sleeping in her spare bedroom.

I did manage to gather a few steamy stories from some of the people I encountered who were having sex in their seventies. One funny story went like this. I was helping a friend of mine rearrange some of her new furniture and in the process, we proceeded to move the sofa to a different location. She said, be careful moving this piece of furniture because on many occasions Dan and I have sex on that sofa. Now, every time I visit my friend Estelle, I picture her and her guy going at it hot and heavy on that sofa. Yes, they are in their seventies.

The sexy seventies is not exclusive to heterosexuals. My gay friends, Bill and Edward, enjoyed a beautiful, long lasting gay relationship for the better part of 25 years. Then Edward got ill, and Bill became his devoted caregiver. They moved into an independent living location in Florida because it would be easier for Bill than to have to maintain their home while caring for Edward. Two years later, Edward died and a couple years after the grieving period Bill tells of his new-found freedom and how it has sparked his sex life. He now refers to himself as a "SLUT" and he openly tells me that he is whoring around all the time and loving it. I do recall that the reason he chose this particular assisted living location was because he claimed to have a lot of gay friends that were residents there. Bill is in his early seventies and his longtime partner Edward was about 15 years older.

Here's another funny story. I was interviewing a woman about her sexual life with her new boyfriend when her young friend who just happened into the restaurant, sat down with us to chat, not knowing what we were talking about. My friend introduced me to Jan. Jan asked what we were talking about. We told her we were talking about ED. Now here's the funny part - she said she had a few friends with Eating Disorders too. Well, we burst out laughing and finally told her we were discussing Erectile Dysfunction. Needless to say, that conversation continued to be interesting.

I have talked to a lot of women while writing this book, but I must say, it is very hard to get a guy to discuss their sexual dalliances they may be having while in their Septuagenarian years. I wonder if I were able to interview more men would they lie about their sex lives as they used to lie when they referred to their sexual prowess while in their early years. Just saying.

I remember about twenty years ago I heard the story about a group of my husband's mother's friends talking at the bridge table about sex. One of the women piped up with this comment and I have been laughing about it ever since. She said to her bridge friends, "I have not had an 'organism' in 20 years." She and her friends were in their seventies at the time this was said.

A lot of sexy senior citizens of the male gender are dancing in the streets over Viagra and the availability of sexy Septuagenarian women in order to fulfill their sexual pleasure, but for the women I am told, their pleasure still comes from being touched in the right way and being held and adored.

With the advent of Viagra, and the late-night TV advertisements for adult sex toys, it has often been proven to be a satisfying time in the sex lives of this age group.

So, if alternatives such as vibrators can be freely talked about on television, why is it so hard for a sexy senior in their seventies to talk about it? I guess it's just the way they were brought up. Most folks in their seventies were brought up during a sex-negative era. They were taught that sex and sexual desire was shameful and the key word in sex education was to practice abstinence until married.

Actually, it is my belief that was the reason for so many divorces with people who are now Septuagenarians. Since they were taught to never "do it" until married – well, you guessed it, they all got married at a young age in order to "do it" and later got the seven-year itch to try it with another partner and thus, eventually got divorced. Just my opinion of course.

In today's world young adults believe it to be natural to try on the shoe to see if it fits before marriage with no stigma attached. So, though we were taught not to have sex before marriage, we Septuagenarians are still programed to think we should not desire sex at our age and especially since we are not married.  It seems as though after a certain age we are not supposed to enjoy sex or talk about it or G-d forbid do "it".  And, the word masturbation still sounds like a dirty word to most Septuagenarians. But the reality is that many 70 somethings are having sex whether it is with a partner or not.

Again, it is very hard to get people to talk about self-satisfaction or "solo sex" as it is often called.  It is a fact that cannot be ignored by the vast number of widows and widowers who are in their seventies. After all, they are not dead yet. I clearly remember several episodes of Sex and the City, a popular TV show, where several of the girls spoke freely of their relationship with their vibrators. Each of the episodes that I can recall were because they were "man less" at that particular stage of their dating life and they chose not to become "sex less".

It is sexually challenging if you're not in a relationship to find ways to reintroduce sex into your life, even if that means going it alone. I have come to learn that sex toys are big business and 70-year olds are no exception for contributing to the success of this business.

Another discovery that I have made in my interviews is the fact that a lot of folks in their seventies nap during the day and that causes them to not be able to sleep thru the night so.... this is what happens. While flicking the remote control looking for something to watch on late night/early morning television some say they have run across a late-night advertisement for sex toys. I followed their lead and on several occasions I have watched with interest at the array of stimulators that are available to both men and women. With the ability to order a sex toy in the privacy of your own home as well as the internet it has become a rather anonymous purchase.

After a certain age we're not supposed to enjoy sex. We don't see much about "senior" sex in magazines or movies; we're sedate, we're grannies, we move slowly – sex isn't made for us. Or so it seems.

Actually, studies show there are many reasons to stay active sexually at any age. I read one study in a senior magazine that to be celibate is not healthy.  It said that about 28 percent of people in their 70s were sexually active. That tells me that a whole bunch of Septuagenarians, about 72 percent of them are not having sex and that is not healthy. As the story goes, having sex with or without a partner would be good for 70 something's general health. Just saying

I learned early on with my interviews that none of the married Septuagenarians were comfortable talking about their sex lives thus the absence of married couple discussions in this chapter. I will leave this area of expertise to the professionals.

Actually, I had the pleasure of meeting a well-known sex therapist better known as the "Dr. Ruth" of Bexley, OH in order to confirm some of what I was talking about in this chapter. Cynthia Leif Ruberg is a Licensed Professional Clinical Counselor who specializes in marital and relationship therapy and sex therapy. Ruberg read this chapter and concurred with what I was saying regarding "the sexy 70-year olds". And, of course I went to her web site and learned more.

So, if you are seventy or plus and are sexually challenged you might want to go to your sandbox and play with your new toys. And, if you have any pieces and parts of this chapter that are not functioning the way you wish then you just might want to find a good "sex therapist". Just saying.

Chapter 11

# From Psychedelic to Psychosomatic

Q: Why should septuagenarians use valet parking?
A: Because valets don't forget where they parked your car.

If you can remember psychedelic art from the sixties and you can't remember where you put your keys, you might be between the ages of 70 – 80.

Some of the late Septuagenarian's I talked to, those from the silent generation especially, have little or no connection to Psychedelic art, or Woodstock or Birkenstocks. And, the Baby Boomer Septuagenarians were forever scarred from the Vietnam War. Unlike the baby boomer Septuagenarians who were dodging the draft, the older 70 something women were dealing with diapers instead of making love and peace in their tie-dyed shirts.

A lot of Septuagenarians are a bit psychosomatic. What is psychosomatic? A psychosomatic disorder is when mental factors cause physical symptoms, but where there is no actual physical disease.

They will complain about their health all the time and you begin to wonder if it is all real or just psychosomatic. Oy Vey, I ache all over you will hear them say. Hmmm.

You might hear everything from my feet hurt, my back hurts, my legs ache, my allergies are acting up, my gut hurts, and a million other ailments. After all my interviews I began to realize that it is impossible to reach your seventies without having at least three specialist doctors located in your speed dial.

A-Fib, stents, arthritis, fibromyalgia, the big C, etc., is common everyday language in the life of 70 something's. Knee replacements, hip replacements, and lower back pain becomes the kvetch of the day. In other words, the 70 something's seemed to complain about any and all of the above on a daily basis. I used to think everyone I met when I was in my early 70s was psychosomatic, however, as I got closer to my 80s I began to realize that a lot of their complaints were real.

Of all the aches and complaints I am hearing from my Septuagenarian friends, the one that worries them most is never being able to find their keys. Yep, you got it. They worry the most about dementia and Alzheimer's disease.

Once you start forgetting where you put your keys, or where you parked your car, you begin to wonder: Am I getting Alzheimer's or am I just getting a little forgetful, or what? You know enough about it to be wary of your own aging process and worry that you too may be getting AD. It gets especially scary if you have had a loved one who suffered from this horrible disease because you may well recognize the signs.

Mindy and Don led a well-ordered life. They were busier in retirement than they had been when they were both working. Life was good, until Don started showing signs of forgetfulness. At first they laughed about it, but as time went on Mindy could see that Don's behavior was troublesome. Finally, after seeing a doctor the proper testing was done and the doctor told them to come BACK IN SIX MONTHS. Six months later the doctor, after having done more testing, was able to diagnose Don with having Alzheimer's disease.

Obviously, this wasn't part of their master plan. They had just downsized and planned to travel and especially traveling to Arizona to spend time with their children.

The terrible news of Don's Alzheimer's hit Mindy hard. She vowed, at this time, to keep Don at home until the end. In his case, the Alzheimer's disease progressed rapidly.

One day he went to meet some friends and got lost going to a place he traveled to on numerous occasions. He called Mindy in bewilderment, explaining that he could not find the place. Of course, she came, and led him home. It became clear to Mindy that it was probably time to take his driving privileges away. It was hard to take this step however other things relating to his Alzheimer's were progressing so fast that it was not as hard to have him give up driving as she thought it would be.

Don's AD was going from bad to worse and as Mindy said, she planned on seeing this through to the end. Don became incontinent, couldn't dress himself, spoke incoherently. She called their sons and they decided she would have to move to Arizona. It was the only way she could keep Don at home. They moved to a 55 and older community and are still there now. Don is still alive, declining rapidly and he is no longer the person she married 54 years ago. All the planning in the world does not prepare you for this.

Many people I talked to said they found themselves having trouble finding the right word and wonder if they are getting Alzheimer's or is this just a product of their age. But, often these kinds of things are just typical age-related changes like forgetting names, then recalling that name later in the day. It's very frustrating, for sure they concurred.

If you get too worried about yourself, or your loved ones, getting dementia/Alzheimer's disease, by all means please get tested. There is a difference between the two and proper diagnosis will determine what meds you might be placed on.

There is an upside when it comes to health in this day and age. We've lived long enough to be blessed with having doctors who specialize in these diseases, oncologists, rheumatologists, neurologists, cardiologists, etc., etc. We are finding out that there are many procedures and medications to treat all that ails us. In fact, the treatments and procedures will very often allow Septuagenarians to become octogenarians and beyond. That is wonderful news in every aspect except for the government having to dole out Social Security incomes over a longer period of time than what was originally thought to be the life span of the population. Because of the aging population the Social Security may not be there for future Septuagenarians.

How many times have you heard the phrase, "Use it or lose it?" Septuagenarians are "using" it in large numbers, thanks to Silver Sneakers, and all of the programs that are geared to seniors at the gyms and recreation centers across the nation. Sandy does a cardio exercise class at the Y one day a week and Silver Splash in the pool twice a week. Kaye, Chuck, Linda, and Barb play Pickleball at the Y three to four times a week and Glenn and Mary are doing a Yoga class at the same Y. Even if you don't get your membership free with Silver Sneakers you probably qualify for a senior discount at any of the many exercise venues that are available.

There is an abundance of 70-year olds with tee times. Bob tells me he can hardly get out of bed in the morning, but he manages to play golf with his buddies every Wednesday. In fact, he said that is his favorite day of the week. They hack their way through 18 holes then go out for lunch and pay up on the bets they made on the course. He said a lot of the guys in the "old farts" league are very wealthy. But, oh do they complain when they lose a quarter on the betting. Bob went on to say he loves this day, not necessarily for the game of golf, but for the comradery he enjoys on that day.

I asked Stuart what he liked about being 70 and he said he loved being able to play in a senior softball league with a bunch of other 70 somethings. I watched a baseball game being played by a bunch of old fogies in Vero Beach, FL, and it was obvious that a lot of these ballplayers were at least 70 and some appeared to be in their eighties. The name of the team was the Codgers – an age appropriate spin off from a name depicting their age and the Brooklyn Dodgers. How appropriate is that?

I interviewed one gentleman who, at the age of 73, still plays soccer every Thursday. It was wintertime and I asked him where he plays soccer in the winter and he says he plays indoor soccer at the local community center. Jan also told me that he does an exercise class similar to Zumba at the same location. Needless to say, Jan had a slim, wiry body that was well taken care of. He told me he was very health conscious.

93

Karin complains about her aching back, yet she and her 80-year old husband play Pickleball four days a week. To make matters even more interesting about this Pickleball couple, her husband is a cancer survivor. Other sports that are being played by active Septuagenarians are tennis, bowling and Tai Chi.

They say it is very important to use the brain, where the "use it or lose it" saying has another meaning other than exercising your aching joints. Seventy somethings are exercising their brains in a lot of ways. Barbie says she loves her brain exercising every morning with her coffee and the newspaper. Before she reads the news, she goes directly to the crossword puzzle. In fact, her newspaper provides her with two crossword puzzles. She said she does one in the morning and moves right into the word scramble, then the cryptogram. Sometimes she gets a brain cramp from these three things, but she feels the need to keep her brain oiled. When evening comes, she glances at the rest of the paper and proceeds to the second crossword puzzle. Another person that I talked to goes directly to the Sudoku game.

Senior centers are a good source for other types of brain activities such as bridge, euchre, and mahjongg. The companionship that the senior crowd gets at these senior centers is priceless. Knitting, quilting, wood carving and drawing classes are some of what is available at most senior centers. A great form of exercise at one senior center is tap dancing. The choices are endless.

One couple, Bob and Joann, had a Friday date at their local senior center every week. They went for the lunch that was served every Friday, and after lunch Joann played bingo while

Bob played ping-pong. Once in a while, when they could not go on a particular Friday, they said there seemed to be a real lonely and bored feeling because of not attending.

I questioned a lot of people in several senior centers and for most the cost of membership was minimal. I found some that were as little as five dollars for a membership to about $45.00 a year. There were some activities that had a slight charge, such as a painting class might have an additional charge of $5.00 for a six-week session. All in all, most seniors found that a membership in a senior center was affordable and enjoyable.

Olive was loving her tap-dancing classes and enjoyed the little dance revue that her senior center put on once a year. She invited her daughter and her granddaughter to attend. She said that once she introduced tap dancing back into her life, when she turned 73, she felt as though she was a kid again. She remembered shuffle ball chain from her tap classes when she was only eleven years old and it was no different at this age. She said the class exercised her brain, her body and improved her balance. It did all of the things she could not get excited about in an exercise class. Olive said the icing on the cake was costuming up for the yearly revue.

When I think of psychedelic art the name Peter Max always comes to mind. The Peter Max Poster Book of Art is a perfect example of the psychedelic art I am speaking of. And, I might add, Peter Max has had staying power as an artist. He was producing works of art during his Septuagenarian years. His paintings are still very much in demand.

So, whether you are from the psychedelic age group in your early 70s or are just plain psychosomatic, you cannot underestimate the phrase of "use it or lose it".

That is exactly what my friend Lucille Borgen did. She used "it" until the day she died at the age of 98.

Lucille became an active tournament water skier when she entered the Ohio State Championships in 1959 at the age of 46, where she won. She went on to win more than 30 national titles and held the U.S. national record in Women 9 (ages 75-79) jumping, slalom and trick skiing.

She stayed in shape by exercising six days a week using weights, doing aerobics and skiing at least three times a week. Lucille survived polio as a child, cancer as an adult and the complete loss of vision in her left eye a few years before the age of 91 when she was still skiing every day near her home in Babson Park, FL. Living in San Ysidro, California at the age of 98 she died on June 8, 2012.

So, bring it on...you're in your seventies. Stay tuned and stay toned.

I guess it does not matter whether you are a baby boomer or if you hail from the silent generation, there seem to be physical and mental activities for everyone. Seventy somethings can exercise their brain, their body and their bones, no matter how they float their boat.

Chapter 12

# What Are You Afraid Of?

If a woman is born in Italy, grows up in England, goes to America and dies in Baltimore, what is she?
Dead.

As you may have guessed, one of the biggest fears for a lot of 70-year olds is the fear of dying.

Since many Septuagenarians are not "tech savvy" enough to get all of their news from the internet a lot of them are still reading the newspaper every day. And, do you know what they read first? Yep, you guessed it. They turn to the obituary page before they take their first sip of coffee. Hey, you know, it's important to see who has died and to read the ages of the newly dead and it is especially important to be the first to know if someone you knew died.

In fact, one of the dreaded beginning phrases of a conversation with 70 somethings is, "Did you hear." That's usually followed by "Did you hear that so and so has died?"

The more I talked to people, the more I began to realize that Septuagenarians have a lot of fears.  Alzheimer's disease rates high on the list of fears for a lot of Septuagenarians followed by strokes and cancer. Losing their eyesight is another fear mentioned by a lot of 70 somethings.

Rebecca sought me out for a discussion about AD one day knowing that my husband had Alzheimer's disease. We chatted for a long time about her fear. First, she told me about her sister who had recently been diagnosed with AD and asked me a lot of questions about how I was able to recognize when my husband was diagnosed. Then she admitted to me that she thought she was getting it. She said she has stopped using her brain and she recognizes herself being forgetful. I told her I am not a doctor and I would be the last person she should ask if she has the signs of AD, however, I did tell her to stop worrying and start doing crossword puzzles and other brain games. That was the best I could do with advice for her.

Most of the people I talked to during the writing of this book seemed to have learned to live one day at a time and they try hard to enjoy each day and not dwell on their fears.

My brother Danny was the fourth in line of the five of us so it was never expected that he would be the first to go. After all, three of us were already Septuagenarians. He died of the dreaded big C. Shortly after my brother's death I lost my husband who had suffered from several strokes and Alzheimer's disease. I was in my mid-seventies at the time. Septuagenarians, especially the older 70-year olds, begin to realize they are surrounded by sickness and death on a regular basis. No wonder they fear death.

The story of Shelley and Randy is sad. They traveled extensively in retirement and were a very loving couple who were living a loving life. Randy was driving home from a meeting one day and his car flipped into the ditch just before he reached his own driveway.  One of his neighbors witnessed the whole event. The neighbor jumped out of his car and found Randy lying unconscious and he immediately called 911. Randy was rushed to the hospital and that was the beginning of a yearlong agony for his wife Shelley. Randy broke his neck, he was paralyzed, had brain damage and was on a feeding tube.

As the story goes, Shelley was pampered by Randy through all their married life and now she was faced with the greatest and gravest challenge.  She rose to the occasion in a big way. She visited Randy every single day and sat with him from morning to evening.  Friends came to visit, she read, spoke to doctors and nurses, and never left his side.  Slowly she realized that all her prayers could not be answered.  He died a year later, and Shelley said that at the time of his death she was finally ready to let him go.

Shelley had a year to prepare herself for the inevitable, but Hilda and Ray's story was much different.  Ray was a macho military man who took charge of everything in their marriage while pampering his beautiful wife. Hilda spent much of her time decorating their home and cooking gourmet dinners with a table set with fine china and silver. Needless to say, Hilda knew nothing of their finances – in fact she told me she never wrote a check and she not only did not know how to balance their checking account, she did not know how much money was in the checking account.

You can well imagine how lost she was when in one single moment Ray keeled over and died from a heart attack. Somehow Hilda managed with the help of their grown children and some close friends. But she was a perfect example of how unprepared for the death of a spouse a person can be.

Actually, Septuagenarians have fears other than dying. The more I talked to people about their fears the more I realized that fear for the 70-year-old woman is much different than what men fear.

Women feared mechanical problems in their home such as an air conditioner or furnace conking out. A broken garbage disposal would send most women into a tizzy. After talking to a good many 70-year old's I found out if you ever needed the name of a good handyman, just call one of your widow friends…. They have a bevy of good handymen on tap for any and all repairs that may be needed. Knowing a good handyman was a sure cure for a lot of women's fears. Just saying.

Car problems are high on the list of fears for a lot of women. Most of the women I talked to were either not aware of OnStar for car emergencies nor did they want to hear about it. They said they will stick with the tried and true services of AAA. And, not surprisingly, men did not share these same fears.

It took a little time to figure out men's fears but the signs were always there. Widowers feared spending the remainder of their years alone. They feared loneliness much more than they feared a mechanical failure or car problems. Now, here is the interesting part of a man's fear of being alone. I found that they feared dating even more. Well, maybe not fear of dating as much as fear of rejection. Several of the women who were dating told me they had to make the first move. I suppose this is because men fear rejection as much as loneliness.

Let me tell you the story about Marci who could not get into her garage one evening after playing mahjongg with her friends. She pushed that remote control three or four times, from many an angle with no success of getting her garage door to open. She parked her car on the street and the next day, after checking with a few of her more knowledgeable friends about what to do she was told to check the battery on the remote. She went to the local hardware store, bought a new battery and had the kind gentleman who waited on her put the battery in. Marci went home with a smile on her face. Oops, she said. It still would not open so she was forced to call a garage door company.

She said she was furious to find that the clerk in the hardware store put the battery in backwards. It took the garage door guy all of two minutes to figure that problem out and it only cost Marci a $79.00 service call for him to tell her that. No wonder women fear mechanical problems.

Other things that are admittedly feared are spiders, mice and lightning.

Right up there with the fear of dying is the fear of falling. The fear of falling on snow and ice is, of course, a Northern thing, so my Florida friends did not fear that as often as my Ohio friends.

Mary Beth had a fall while out West visiting her daughters and she fell and chipped the bone in her knee. She came back to Ohio with a walking cast and was out of commission for her regular activities for about two months. She was one of those working Septuagenarians and could not go back during that time. Her daughters bugged her and cajoled her and more or less insisted she get one of those "Help me – I fell and can't get up" necklaces so she finally did get one. I asked her if she wears it and she said when she is in her home she puts it on, but she does not wear it when she goes out. I guess that is better than nothing.

One lady told me the story of her friend Patti who was always falling and tripping. Apparently when she was out shopping with her visiting daughter she tripped and took quite a bad fall. She blamed it on her new "wedgie" shoes. That was perhaps one of four recent falls that she had taken, some being pretty bad, so the neighbors began to talk. She told me they had suspected Patti was falling because she was drunk. Drinking and walking, especially in high heeled shoes can be tough when you're in your 70s. Just saying.

One of the most mentioned fears I was hearing about was the fear of being a burden to their loved ones. Septuagenarians were very expressive about not wanting to be a burden...to their children, their spouse etc. They did not want to be a burden financially, physically and most of all mentally.

The funniest response I got when asking about fears was from one 70-year-old who shall remain anonymous, even in this format. She said she feared farting while on a date. That got a big chuckle out of me.

All in all, the better part of all the people I talked to during the writing of this book seemed to be living one day at a time and enjoying each day and not dwelling on their fears.

Chapter 13

# What Is Your "Exit Strategy"?

Two old men sitting on a park bench.

Jesse: Do you know why I am looking forward to moving to that assisted living place?

Herman: No, why?

Jesse: Because there are five women to every man.

New hi-rise condos were being built overlooking the golf course at the Country Club where Cathy hangs out. She went to the preview presentation given to members of the club where attendees were offered a sizeable discount to members of the Club if they would sign up for a unit within one month of the presentation – during the pre-construction phase.

Cathy told me it got her thinking. Maybe this is where I should be she thought. She started checking off the pros and cons of taking advantage of this pre-construction deal. The square footage is more than she now has in her free-standing home so downsizing would not be necessary. Cathy tells me that she actually has what a lot of folks would say is the perfect house for a single person of her age. Her house is all one floor, 2 car attached garage and is conveniently located in an upscale neighborhood.

She said she talked to her children on two separate phone calls about the possibility of putting her house on the market and moving into one of these new high rises overlooking the golf course and the clubhouse. From the immediate argumentative tone of her children, it was very apparent that they were against what she was contemplating, in fact, so much so that they did not give her much chance to argue her points.

Both of Cathy's sons told her what a loser financially this would be for her. One son kept saying, you need to keep your eye on the "exit strategy" and that this purchase would make her exit strategy a real loser financially. You know, they argued, that homes such as hers would sell much easier than a condo – blah, blah, blah. They kept repeating the word "exit strategy" because it would be harder getting rid of a condo than to sell her house if she were to have to go to an assisted living facility.

As Cathy's story unraveled, I began to think the term "exit strategy" had some teeth to it so I interviewed others about this very issue. Most of the people I interviewed, especially those in their mid to late 70's, began to wonder where they might be living out their remaining years.

Linda's story: Linda lived in a beautiful condominium surrounded by a golf course view on one side and a ravine on the other side. Her condo consisted of about 28 hundred square feet of living space with three levels of stairs. One year after her husband passed away Linda started to have a few health problems herself and became dependent on using a walker. She told me that she could almost make do by taking her time and holding on to the railing to navigate the stairs to go to bed. However, going down the stairs became a real challenge. She found that the only way she could get down the stairs was to scoot down the stairs on her butt. Once the stairs became an issue her two daughters stepped in. They thought it best for her to sell the condo and move into an independent living facility. She found a very nice facility, moved in and it did not take her long to realize that she was not happy there. She missed her old condo and her old neighbors and did not like living in this "new" location. She said she thought the others living there we so old and so much more incapacitated than she, that she was not comfortable with them. She was thinking of her "exit strategy" because she could not navigate the stairs in her old place.

Essie's story: Essie lived in a condo that had high condo fees and very high utility bills. She was in a large upscale community that had a pool and a party house. Due to some very bad business decisions her late husband made, she found it necessary to continue to work and knew full well that she could not afford her life style once she found herself not able to work. In fact, she barely made ends meet with a full-time job. After a year or so of thought she finally bit the bullet and put her condo on the market. Downsizing and finding a place that she could afford became her challenge. Essie got lucky. She sold her expensive condo in one day and found another smaller condo about one mile away for less money and less monthly expenses than what she was dealing with. In fact, she told me that the sale and the move was about to save her close to $800 each month. I asked her why she bought another condo –why did she not just take the money from the sale of her larger place and just rent? If she rented she would have no maintenance, no condo fees and she could let the landlord have all the headaches. She knew she would have to work for most of her remaining years as long as she stayed healthy, however if she ever found herself needing additional income to put a roof over her head and was not able to work, she would take a reverse mortgage on the new place. So, a reverse mortgage was her "exit strategy."

Dvora's story: Dvora spent a lot of time without any of her friends knowing what was going on in her home. She was downsizing quietly and giving things away. She gave some things to her grandchildren and some things she sold at the neighborhood garage sales. She said that she was able to get herself to the point where she thought maybe there was the possibility that she might be able to seamlessly enact her "exit strategy". She came to understand that her only child would not be able to help her when she would need him, nor was he capable. She said he was barely able to function in his own little world with his own dysfunctional wife. As Dvora said, she worked with her financial advisor and her attorney, set up her trust fund and quietly shopped for a place to settle down after 40 years in her present location. She was able to find an independent living facility in the part of town that she knew so well. She put a deposit on a brand-new senior living facility, a one-bedroom apartment with a full kitchen and then put her home on the market. Within two months' time she was situated in her new home and was thrilled to be settled. She said it was the best thing she has ever done and will rest comfortably that she is situated for the rest of her life. She can go from independent living, to assisted living, to memory care if needed and skilled nursing all at the same facility so......the rest is up to her. It was a fairly expensive way to go but she came to the conclusion that was what her money was for. Dvora said she is able to maintain her usual friendships and social life and the new location has also opened up a plethora of new friends and activities. She said she is one happy camper. The best part of her move according to our discussion was that she is no longer lonely. She is surrounded by the residents and activities while still maintaining her long-time friendships.

Becca's story:  Becca, a recent widow, lived in a small three-bedroom home in a nice neighborhood with little or no expenses. The house was paid for and her car was paid for but, it was still a house and with that responsibility comes expenses. There were taxes, insurance, HOA fees, and always some unforeseen maintenance, however her children were nearby and could always be counted on for help. Soon family chatter told her that they would not always be around. One son traveled extensively out of the country and had a second home in another state and her daughter and her husband were starting to talk about putting their house up for sale and moving into a cabin in the woods about 1 ½ hours from her. The reality of her situation, as she was pushing thru the better part of her seventies was that her life line with her children was slowly slipping away. After having the comfort of knowing they were nearby most of the time (within eight miles of her house) Becca was facing the fact that she was going to be alone at the time when she had always assumed they would be there for her. An independent living facility would probably be her next move she said. The only problem was, when should you make this decision? When should she begin the process of implementing her "exit strategy?" She was 75 years old, healthy, and maintained a very active social life and knew she was not yet ready to start planning for her final move. All the facilities she knew of and looked at seemed to be habituated by a bunch of old people and she was not ready to face that yet.

Most everyone I talked to, when faced with an "exit strategy" of any kind, said "you had better be prepared to be able to make that decision on your own and to leave yourself in a situation that you will be independent of your children." Most everybody that I interviewed agreed that their children will not be willing nor able to stick around and be there for you when you need them.

Patsy and Chuck had a real problem regarding their "exit strategy". They were getting up there in years and began to realize an independent living facility where several of their friends were settling in was the place they should be. They figured out their daily expenses and concluded they were spending almost as much to live day to day, month to month in their home than what it would cost them to live in such a facility. They figured what they were spending at the grocery store would just about cover the expenses of the meal plan. The upkeep was nil, and housekeeping was included. They were ready but, they could never get to this "carefree" lifestyle because they did (in their minds) a very stupid thing. They did a reverse mortgage on their home about three years previously and their home no longer belonged to them. It belonged to the bank. They were not able to sell the house and use the equity as a down payment for the assisted living facility. In other words, because of the reverse mortgage the bank was now the owner of their home. Their "exit strategy" was foiled due to the reverse mortgage.

I got to wondering what older people in other countries do as an "exit strategy" and did a little research on this topic. In Japan, many families have several generations living under one roof. It is thought to be one reason they live longer in Japan than any other population. There are actually more elderly people in Japan than there are young people. Think of the advantages of many generations under one roof. The young ones work and have children. The older generation cooks and cleans and babysits. Wow, why don't we live like this in our country? It would also be a much better living situation than living alone and footing the bill of living alone, but I am sure our kids would not like this kind of living situation.

Life on a Kibbutz in Israel is nothing more than communal living. People of every age group live together and share the work load. Mixing a little of that and a little of the Japanese families who live together with several generations just might be a new way to go in this country. Just saying.

The recurring theme of all the folks I talked to was that while they were in their 70s they did not particularly want to come to grips with their "exit strategy". For the most part, they realized that assisted living facilities were for old people and they still did not feel old and living with their grown children and their grandchildren was probably not going to happen with most of the people I talked to. So, most of them just chugged along, living day to day in the best way they could.

Though an "exit strategy" looms in the mind of the older Septuagenarians, most of them will be putting this stage of their lives on the back burner until it becomes a real necessity.

It is hard growing old and harder yet to try to figure out your own "exit strategy". As they say, growing old is not for sissies. Only you can make the right decision for yourself while you are still of sound mind and body.

Chapter 14

# Self-Serve…The New Method of Modern Madness

A man walks into a bookstore and asks the clerk if she could tell him where the "self-help" area is.

She replied, "Of course I can, but that would defeat the purpose, now wouldn't it?"

You can't write about 70-year olds without hearing the phrase…"I remember when." There was no such thing as self-serve way back when, so, let's get started.

We remember when every gas station had at least one gas station attendant. All you did was roll down the window, not an electric window I might add, and they would ask you what you need. "Give me a dollar's worth or fill-er-up" I might answer. The attendant would then pump your gas, wash your windows and put air in your tires as a service. It was the worst day in my life when I realized that service was not going to be available to me anymore. Now I have to pump my own gas.

Those of us born in the silent generation – 1925-1945 may recall the price of gas when pulling into the station. When we were lucky enough to borrow Dad's car to cruise the local drive-in restaurant on Friday nights we all chipped in 10 cents to gas up the car. That 10 cents was good for a lot of cruising.

The average price of gasoline in 1930 was 12 cents per gallon, 1940 20 cents, 1950 30 cents, and 1960 45 cents per gallon. The boys who were born into the "silent generation" spent their gasoline money doing drag racing. Who says things are better today? What would you rather have, a gas station attendant washing your windows and pumping your gas, or do you like to stand out there in the freezing rain or the hot sun doing it yourself? Is this progress?

You are hardly able to buy groceries these days by going thru the checkout line. They have converted most checkout lines to the "do it yourself" method.... self-serve. Wake up folks, this is not being done for your convenience. Once this industry teaches the shoppers to check themselves out, they see the day when they can eliminate check out personnel.

Dottie talked about shopping for a dress for a special occasion at an upscale department store. She took a few dresses into the fitting room and began the process. One dress was too tight so she wanted to try it on in the next size up. Not a salesperson in sight she told me. That was when we began the discussion of what it used to be like to shop in the department stores. Back then, your salesperson took great pleasure in helping you with your selections and if you needed another in a different size she was right there to get it for you. That is not the way it is today. If you needed another size or another color you would have to dress again, go back to the rack where you found that dress and look for one in that next size up or a different color. Then, it's back to the fitting room, undress so that you can try it on to see if it will be a better fit. Dottie also recalled the day when the salesperson in the dress department kept a personal file on her and she would receive a call when something came in that she might like or need. Those days are gone forever.

After you have dealt with the challenge of finding what you are ready to purchase in any upscale department store the next challenge is to pay for it. Cash registers are hard to find and most "pay stations" are not necessarily conveniently located to your purchase item. When you do finally locate a check out station chances are you will stand in a long line to complete your purchase. Shopping in a fine department store is no longer a pleasurable experience say most of the Septuagenarians I interviewed. They only have fond memories of what it used to be like.

Remember when you used to go to the bank, and you could go up to the window where a teller would take care of you. Hmmm. There are very few tellers these days. Again, self-serve is the method of madness. You no longer have the convenience and the personal help of the teller because you are now doing most of your banking at a machine called ATM outside of the bank -   either a walk up or drive through window. ATM, an automated teller machine is yet another form of self-serve rearing its ugly head.

I personally try to go into the bank when I need cash because my arms are too short to navigate my way through the prompts on the drive through window or I forgot my pin number as has often been the case. Most Septuagenarians I talked to have fond memories of going to the bank way back when. Many of us can remember being taken to the bank by our parents and getting our 10-cent deposit recorded in our little blue bank book. It taught us to be savers and a good many 70-year olds have retained that habit of saving.

We have come to realize that we must help ourselves to gasoline for our cars, cash from an ATM machine, checking out our groceries, and shopping for that special dress in the department store. We are even learning how to help ourselves to psychiatry via the internet. Just ask Google and you can get all the self help you need.

Making a telephone call is another form of self-serve. You are expected to navigate your way to the person or department you want to speak to by listening carefully and punching in button number one or button number two blah blah blah. If you miss or do not understand the prompt, they will play it over. This process usually extends a three-minute phone call to twenty minutes.... of course, that is if you asked for them to speak in English.

Self-diagnosed doctoring on Web MD is another form of self-help with no credentials to confirm if you have arrived at the cause of your medical problem. This can be a dangerous form of doctoring and that is not the way to take care of yourself because you chose to do a self-help session on Web MD. Just saying.

Chapter 15

# The Brotherhood of Widowhood

A man attends the funeral of an old friend.

He sees the grieving widow and asks if he could say a word. The widow allows it, and the man stands up and yells, "PLETHORA!"

The widow looks up at him and with a smile says, "Thank you that means a lot."

**H**ow do you feel about living alone I asked during some of my interviews? Annie went on to tell me she has never lived alone until recently when her husband passed away. She recalled she lived with her siblings and parents then married her husband. She lived with her husband and then with her husband and children.  When the children left the nest, she shared her life and home with her husband until he passed away. She was a Septuagenarian when her husband passed, and she went on to tell me that for the first time in her life she was living alone- really alone.

It took some getting used to say many of the people I talked to. Hanging with some of their longtime friends and meeting new friends and staying busy was the formula for living alone. Some of these women are convinced they will live alone for the remainder of their lives. Not so for many men. There is a saying that goes something like this…when there is a death in a marriage, women mourn, and men replace.

Men seemed to have more trouble with living alone. Take grocery shopping for instance. They tend to shop with a list more often than their female counterparts. Men stick to basics like bread, lunch meat and milk and like to garnish this meal with potato chips. Women would be more apt to buy canned tuna and make a tuna salad for lunch. I was able to talk to a few men regarding their culinary expertise and Joe told me he made a mean chili. A lot of men deemed themselves very proficient on the grill however, if asked if they like to cook, they say they cook rather than starve.

Chuck, whose wife passed away about two years ago, says he plays a lot of golf but does not make any effort for other kinds of activities. I asked him what he does when he is not playing golf. He said he hangs around the house and watches television. Chuck goes out to eat about three or four times a week and usually fixes himself a sandwich and a beer for dinner when he eats at home.

Widowhood is very hard on the newly widowed spouse. It takes time to sort out your feelings – everything from sorrow to loneliness and anger and in some cases relief.

I talked to several 70 somethings who had been caregivers for spouses with Alzheimer's, myself included. Most of the stories were similar – it was sad, it was lonely, and most of all we all spoke of the loss of our partner as a lingering experience. It was a form of widowhood before widowhood actually occurred.

The more I ventured into trying to understand and write about widowhood I began to realize I was getting most of my stories from widows, not widowers. It was hard to find men who were willing to talk about being alone after their spouse's death. I did not know or run into very many men who were widowers and I did not know how to reach out to men for answers to my questions about this subject so…the idea came to me. Why not join an on-line dating site and maybe I would meet and be able to communicate with this particular group of men? Well, that is exactly what I did. And, if you will recall I talked about on-line dating in an earlier chapter before I joined up for research purposes.

About two weeks into this on-line dating venture, I began to see patterns. The most glaring thing I discovered was that widowed men were looking for a wife. First and foremost, I was reading in their profiles that a majority of them were looking for a serious relationship and marriage. I continued to talk to the female widows about this fact and most told me that even though they would like to meet a man they almost unanimously stated they were not looking to remarry.

It occurred to me that while 70 somethings were in college way back when, a lot of the gals were looking to get their MRS. degree and now I am starting to realize that 70 something widowed men are looking to get a new "husband" license. My how the worm has turned.

I copied from two different profiles with my on-line dating site and here are two comments made by two different men. "I would love to have someone to spend my life with" and "I am looking for a long-term relationship or hopefully marriage."

Again, I will tell you that is not the way the widows (women) were thinking.

Some guys answered the profile question what are you looking for by saying I am looking for a long-term relationship, or marriage, or a friendship or a pen-pal.

Now, think about that. What is this guy really saying? Is he looking for a pen-pal, a friendship, marriage or what? I finally got disgusted with this answer after reading many profiles on this on line dating site. Many of the men were giving the same response, so I finally messaged one of them with sarcasm. I said, "Hey bud, what are you looking for? You are confusing me. Are you looking for a marriage, a pen- pal a long-term relationship or what?" I further went on to say, when you can come up with an answer, instead of being all over the place I might want to chat with you. I told him in my message I believe relationships should start with a friendship and that unless they are willing to get to know me as a friend first, I am not interested. Needless to say, I never heard back from that dude. I certainly got a chuckle over my response to him.

So, what are women looking for if they could put it in writing on their own profile on a dating site? Since I was not reading female profiles, I decided to ask this question of some of my female widowed friends. To put it bluntly, some are just looking for a Saturday night dinner date and that is all. Of course, some of the widows whom I interviewed would like to have a serious relationship but most who I talked to were not interested in re-marrying nor did they ever want to take care of an aging man.

That remark probably stems from many who have been through the caregiver routine and care not to have to do it again. I concur.

There are a lot of things for widows to occupy themselves with. As I have said in a previous chapter. There are Church groups, senior centers with loads of activities and plenty of sports activities they can join but there will never be an activity to cure loneliness other than the involvement of another human being.

That is why I am finding the dating sites for seniors not only experimental and informational for this book but hopeful that there might be someone special out there for all of us. It is important for our health to stay socially involved even if it is through the computer. Just saying.

I'm also finding slim pickings on the dating site that I joined, and I refuse to add any additional costs to this experiment. They suck you in for one price then if you want to see who reads your profile or if you want to message and talk to someone you need to pay additional monthly fees. No, that is not for me. I'm not that interested.

Speaking of slim pickings, I was wondering what is the ratio of widowed women to widowed men so I googled that question. Here are some facts that Google spit out to me.

Widow women are joiners. For example, they might join a Mahjongg group or a book club, a quilting bee or an art class. Widowers, (men) tend not to want to join in as much. I noticed there is a significant group of regular widowed women who attend Friday night services at the Temple where I attend. On the same thought, I do not notice many men attending and socializing at Friday night services. Are there really that many more women in widowhood than men?

My research tells me there are more than 13.7 million widowed persons in the United States, over 11 million of these being women. (American Association of Retired Persons 2001) Female survivors have been outdistancing their male counterparts by a continually widening margin and now represent approximately 80 percent of the widowed population in the United States. In 1940 there were twice as many widows as widowers; by 1990 the ratio of widows to widowers had climbed to more than 4 to 1. This ratio is expected to widen in the future.

It would be hard to find out if any of your old female classmates or girlfriends are widows because of not knowing their last names if they had married and had taken on their husbands' last name. I think that is why finding out such facts about men seem to be a bit easier.

I was talking to my sister on the phone about her 60th class reunion. She mentioned a name of one of her old flames and said she thought she heard he died. I said, let me look him up. Well, sure enough, his obituary came up, so it was confirmed that he did indeed pass away. Since my sister does not even own a computer, she was shocked and amazed that I could just google a name and find this kind of information. I did go on to read the obituary of her old flame and we entertained ourselves for the next half hour "googling" names of people we went to school with. As I said, most female names could not be googled.

I began formulating Bring It On...We're in our 70's after moving back to Ohio while caregiving for my ailing husband. The actual writing of the book began during my widowhood and that is why I am ending the book with this chapter called The Brotherhood Of Widowhood.

Why would I want to write about 70-year olds you ask? Well, both of my parents died at a young age and I never thought I would live to be 70. My father was 35 years old when he died, and my mother passed away about 20 years later. That is the reason I began to conceptualize writing about this milestone in my life and the lives of others.

By the time widowhood hit me with the passing of my husband, I started to put into words the things I was learning about myself and my friends who were in their seventies. It's been an adventure that I am glad to have had the opportunity to share with you.

I thought there was no better way to end this book about Septuagenarians than to write about widowhood. We've been through childhood, parenthood and now a lot of 70-year olds are facing widowhood.

Let's face it, widowhood is here to stay. And, as I said in the opening chapter, "We all know what the alternative is."

# Acknowledgements

I would like to acknowledge those who have helped me with various stages of assistance while writing this book in no particular order:  Dolly Conkle, I David Cohen, Tirtzah Sandor, Cynthia Lief Ruberg, Maxine Weinberg, Nancy Hauck, Milt Thomas, Ron and Mary Reitenour, Phil Edelsberg of Edelsberg Photography, Sandy and Dick Rose, Nellie Nagy, Jacky Phillips and the hundreds of people who I interviewed both directly and indirectly during the process. I am forever grateful for their support and their encouragement.

Thanks to my husband's son Darren Blum and Chetena Denora for the beautiful front and back cover of the book. Their combined expertise in the wonderful world of design helped to shape the cover of my book, especially since we used a picture of an oil on canvas that I painted in 1968 as the backdrop.

I want to thank my sons, Glen and Bill for allowing me to bore them incessantly about parts of the book that they certainly had no interest in hearing about. My sister Ruth and big brother Bob played a part by encouraging me to press on when I thought I could not do so.

And, a special heartfelt thanks to Jim Lifter, my editor, for pushing me to the finish line. Without his dedication and patience this book could never have been published.

*Authors note: This book is a work of nonfiction. The names of the persons who have been interviewed during the writing of this book have been changed and or disguised.

# Acknowledgements

# About the Author
## Bea Gardner

Like Grandma Moses, Gardner got her start writing late in life while writing her popular Blog called Bea-isms. Prior to her blog, her painting and sculpting classes led Bea to a very successful career as an Interior Designer. Bea still defines herself as an Interior Designer and writing as her hobby.

She began formulating **"Bring It On – We're In Our 70's"** after moving back to Ohio during her years as caregiver for her ailing husband.

Bea was born in Canton, Ohio and spent most of her childhood in Cleveland. She lived in Vero Beach, FL for 25 years and now resides in New Albany, OH.

Contact Information
e-mail: **bea@beagardner.com**
**www.beagardner.com**